SOMALIS
In Search of Nationhood, Statehood and Transnational Connections

Adonis & Abbey Publishers Ltd
St James House
13 Kensington Square,
London, W8 5HD
United Kingdom

Website: http://www.adonis-abbey.com
E-mail Address: editor@adonis-abbey.com

Nigeria:
Suites C4 & C5 J-Plus Plaza
Asokoro, Abuja, Nigeria
Tel: +234 (0) 7058078841/08052035034

Copyright 2016 © A. Osman Farah

British Library Cataloguing-in-Publication Data
A catalogue record for this book is available from the British Library

ISBN: 978-1-909112-57-5

The moral right of the author has been asserted

All rights reserved. No part of this book may be reproduced, stored in a retrieval system or transmitted at any time or by any means without the prior permission of the publisher

SOMALIS
In Search of Nationhood, Statehood and Transnational Connections

A. Osman Farah

Acknowledgements

This research is the product of theoretical considerations and empirical work that took about four years. More than one hundred people contributed to this outcome in the following ways; accepting interview requests, reading and commenting on early drafts, suggesting alternative ideas as well as giving critiques that reshaped my original ideas. I cannot be able mention them all but I am sincerely grateful to their understanding and support.

Particular gratitude to my colleagues at Development and International Relations, Department of Culture and Global Studies - Aalborg University, who provided critical ideas and exchange on potential possibilities and development for the work. I owe gratitude to the contributions made during the seminars and group sessions we co-organized that gave valuable input to the formulation of various chapters. I cannot forget to thank Professor Peter Hervik who often had time to exchange and discuss ideas on culture, international media and global development.

Professor Ali Jimale Ahmed at Queens College and the CUNY Graduate Center, New York, Professor Abdi Kusow at Iowa State University, and Professor Ananta Giri of Madras Institute of Development Studies, India provided invaluable suggestions and comments to earlier versions of some of the chapters. Michael Omondi Owiso at the Political Science Department, Aalborg University provided insightful comments. Professor Hongbing Chen facilitated travel and stay at North-Western University, Shenyang, China. In the same vein Professor Chunrong Liu, School of International Relations and Public Affairs, Fudan University, China, supported the research work in China and facilitated connections to colleagues and networks at Fudan University and Shanghai. A friend and former colleague at our department Dr Juian Zhang hosted me at the School of Government, Beijing Normal University, China. I would also like to thank communities in the Arabian Gulf and in the Horn of Africa for supporting the research that led to this book – particularly during the field work. In the Horn of Africa I benefitted from scholars I met and interviewed at Amoud, Mogadishu and Banadir Universities. Many of these scholars remained in Somalia and with limited resources and under extreme challenges succeeded in establishing high quality educational institutions that contribute not just to human capabilities development and progress in Somalia, but also in the Horn of Africa region and beyond.

Similarly, I would like to appreciate the often enthralling and remarkably enriching SSIA congresses which, in recent years respectively took place in Oslo, Norway and Helsinki, Finland. Particularly colleagues in Finland immensely contributed to diverse inspirational and encouraging activities such as publications and network creations in relation to Somali and Horn of African studies.

The research for some of the chapters in this book were made possible by generous support from the Department of Culture and Global Studies, Aalborg University; Nordic Fudan Centre in Shanghai China, North-Western University, Shenyang, China and different transnational NGOs that supported the field work process.

I am also grateful to Professor John Clammer of the United Nations University, Tokyo, Japan and Professor Mohamed Salih of international Institute of Social Studies (ISS) and Erasmus University Rotterdam; Netherlands. Both of them have been supportive in my research and publications.

List of Acronyms

TC	Transnational Communities
TNGOs	Transnational NGOs
NGO	Non-governmental organizations
Oxfam	Oxfam Committee for Famine relief
AA	Action Aid
G8	Eight country member Economic Organization
G20	Twenty country member Economic Forum
UNICEF	United Nations Children's Fund
NOVIB	Netherland Organization for International development Organization
AU	African Union
UN	United Nations
IMO	The International Migration Organization
BRICS	Brazil, Russia, India, China and South Africa
UAE	United Arab Emirates
EU	European Union
DPP	Danish People's Party
SSIA	Somali Studies International Association
UK	United Kingdom

Table of Contents

Acknowledgements IV

List Of Acronyms VI

Introduction
Transnational Communities and The Transformation of Nation And State 9

Chapter One
The Justice of Improving Security and Confronting Poverty: The Role of
Transnational NGOs and Communities 31

Chapter Two
Transnational Civil Society: Contribution To Development And Security 63

Chapter Three
Balancing National And Transnational Networking Activities:
The Case of Amoud University 85

Chapter Four
Civil Society, Transnational Communities and Political Discourse 103

Chapter Five
Balancing Constructive Development With Material and Human Resources:
Transnational Community Perspectives on Brics 119

Chapter Six
Transnational Citizenship, Violence, Extremism and International Aid 141

Chapter Seven
Transnational Community Consolidation And Mobilization: The Case of
Transnational Somali Communities in The Uae 173

Chapter Eight
From Civilizational Clash to Welfare Eligibility: Ethnic Community
Perspectives on Danish Coalitions 201

Bibliography 227

Index 258

INTRODUCTION

Transnational communities and the transformation of nation and state

This book contains a selection of the author's original research since 2012. The work reflects multiple research activities and contributions to diverse academic activities, including teaching sessions, conducting fieldwork and participating in workshops and conferences in Africa, Europe, China and the Middle East. The work aims to bring diverse and comparative scholarship derived from different countries and locations together under the common theme of nationhood, statehood and transnational connections. The different chapters explore the common idea that transnational activities and connections made by transnational communities originating from the Horn of Africa– particularly by Somalis–represent a new form of socio-political transformation in the processes of understanding the contemporary complexities of development, nationhood and statehood. In our current complex, globalised world, ethnic communities link to multiple socio-economic and political fields. This includes the question of being liveliness; and the dialectic fusion of the symbolic and the manifest, the praxis that combines ritual and chronicle, and how they are recast to help a community's psychic and physical activities. Such activities have regained relevance in debates about the processes of transnational and global development. These are the processes Alain Touraine (2007), in his call for a 'New Paradigm for Understanding Today's World' describes that 'We are now living through the undermining of national communities and strengthening of ethnic communities'. Touraine refers not to old primordial form of social relations but rather a new conflict between state and marked-centred forces against new and creative forms of social movements (Touraine, 2007: 208-10). The presence of transnational communities and their actions and interconnected relations through multiple locations attest to their pursuit of an alternative developmental approach rather than the static and often linear developmental propositions of belonging and operating within the confines of a singular nation and state. Transnational activities in the past privileged the state that, through coercive and consensual power, engaged in both national and transnational relations. Similarly, transnational corporations assert structures of 'complex interdependency' in multiple locations (Koahane and Nye, 2011: 20-21). These forms of transnational relations take the nation and the state as the point of departure in analysis. This book considers transnational communities as the primary vehicle in understanding the dynamics and dialectics of transnational connections. Such communities are in their transnational interactions more flexible are lesser constrained by bureaucratic and institutional constrains.

'The consolidation of justice and power' (Chapter 1) considers the relationship between justice and power in Somalia. The two concepts remain fundamental in general and in particular for current efforts in society- and state-building in Somalia. It is only through the practice of fairness, justice and balanced power-sharing among major social and political actors that Somali society can move forward. Without the fulfilment of basic conditions under which both the weaker and the more powerful feel they are being treated equally and share ownership under the law, it will be difficult to achieve significant political and developmental gains. The problem is that in Somalia, justice and power-sharing is not only an internal issue. The process has been complicated by colonialism, dictatorship and recent transnational complexities. This chapter results from fieldwork in Europe, the Middle East and the Horn of Africa, and attempts to explain the reasons behind the conflict in Somalia and the challenges involving justice and power. Reflections on recent socio-political and historical transformations could help us better understand and explain the dialectics of injustices and power sharing mechanisms– or, rather, the lack thereof – in the country. Equally significant is the reflection of the transnational, not just in terms of different transnational actors engaged in peace- and state-building enterprises in the Horn of Africa, but also in the attempts by different actors within and beyond Somalia to project their own version of justice and power.

Chapter 2, 'Transnational civil society: The contribution to development and security', considers the perspective of transnational communities that engage and develop diverse spaces and locations in diverse multiple forms. In classical times, let us here say during Europe's industrialization in 19th century, civil society was often concentrated within the limits of the local, comprising nation and state construction. Clearly, in today's world the situation is more complex, as transnational communities often simultaneously link and contribute to the developments of multiple locations and localities, thanks to advancements in technology and communications.

Chapter 3, 'Balancing national and transnational networking activities: The case of Amoud University', focuses on transnational regional educational development by examining the role of civil society, particularly the ulama (scholars) and elders, in engaging reconciliation processes in a civil war torn society. In Somalia, scholars and elders have jointly created institutions that prevent wars and advance education and community empowerment. Though not elaborated in this chapter such traditional institutions initially failed in the face of a brutal and nasty civil war. In the outbreak of civil conflict society should put in place mechanisms that could help diffuse tensions among groups and groupings. Successive regimes and warlord minions, however, manipulated the system to their own advantage. The case of Amoud University represents a local initiative that successfully advanced transnational regional education and youth empowerment. These are generations that could not access higher education, due to state collapse and civil war. Such bottom-up community transnational education and peace-building initiatives differ from the often unsuccessful top-down state- and elite-centred securitisation and militarisation activities. As Ferguson (2006: 26) suggests, such local-transnational dynamics remain complex, but it is possible for such groups to navigate from the local to diverse governance 'topographies' that dominate current attempts at global governance. In search of alternative approaches to building nationhood and statehood, Amoud University and other Somali universities represent successful examples of how the local can be connected to the transnational for inclusive benefits. This is a process that can save the country from decades of devastating civil wars and disasters while directing the attention of the people towards educational empowerment and development.

Chapter 4, 'Civil society and political discourse', argues that, in order for a country or a state to properly function, it is necessary for that country to have cohesive horizontal linkages among its citizens. This is also vital for institution-building and consolidation. In particular, fostering positive motivation towards each other and towards public institutions is crucial. This horizontal bonding can, according to Taylor (2011: 124-

125), come first from an individual or group motivation to contribute and be an active part of a society. Secondly, there is a need for open and reasonably free discourse or deliberations in society. Thirdly, societies need to be able to trust in the current and potential members of the concerned political or social community. These processes obviously require the engagement of civil society and the use of formal language as a medium to communicate. In Somalia, there is a clear need to reinvent both national and a transnational civil society and to introduce a discourse of tolerance.

Chapter 5, 'Balancing constructive development with material and human resources: Transnational community perspectives on emerging economies', argues that development is not just an issue of aid and the need to link to the local, national and transnational civil societies; it also requires interrogating who will undertake such transnational links and with whom. In recent years, there has been increased transnational mobility, not just in traditional south-north connections, but also renewed and emerging forms of south-south linkages. Community actors that engage such new transnational linkages include students and business entrepreneurs. These transnational actors link to emerging economies such as China that some see as behaving in a less conditionality-oriented way. For instance both China and India are among countries Africans perceive are friendly and neutral compared to their western counterparts. Many believe that these countries can change the course of the vicious circle of underdevelopment and subordination inherited from colonialism. An obvious candidate to play such a role is China. The problem, however, is that the Chinese state does not directly deal with critical civic associations and organisations that some refer to as a 'civil society'. Nonetheless, transnational communities have somehow– even in less ideally democratic systems, such as in China–managed to organise, more or less formally, to link to multiple locations through educational and business enterprises. This chapter resulted from research that focused on emerging global changes since China became a global economic power. The study looked at how many Africans and African Scandinavians live in China and what social and economic activities these communities are involved with; asking and examining how they are organised in their student and private business enterprises, for example. The study helps us understand the impact of emerging powers on international order and mobility. It also considers whether this economic transformation generates new social mobilisation (movements, organisations) and new transitional social groups/elites and potential novel interactions.

Chapter 6, 'Transnational Citizenship', explores the ways in which citizenship has changed in our current world due to mobility, transfers and many other social, political and economic transformations that make people link not just to one country but also to different countries and locations. During the time of Aristotle and classical times citizenship was linked to the city-state (the polis) and was reserved for men who owned property in the city of Athens. During the Westphalian era, the term citizenship came to reflect increasing nationalism and the construction of new nations and states. In the current world, particularly in many western countries, citizenship has been increasingly linked to the challenges of migration and ethnic minorities –at least in the public debate, and particularly in relation to the acquisition of citizenship. This chapter deals with the transformation of citizenship and how transnational communities aim at complex forms of citizenship rather than the static ones that reflect limited citizenship links to presumed nations and states.

Chapter 7,'Transnational community consolidation and mobilisation: The case of transnational Somali communities in the UAE', presents a case study of how transnational communities address multi-dimensional challenges. These challenges originate not only from the homeland but also from the countries in which these people reside. For instance, communities cope with challenges such as precarity (uncertainties and exclusion related to employment and residence) in the different locations where they find themselves.

Chapter 8, 'From civilizational clash to welfare eligibility: Ethnic community perspectives on Danish coalitions', portrays ethnic communities, including the Somalis in Denmark, in which individuals insist on rejecting the opportunity to become second-class citizens in their adapted homelands. This is often a status uncritically and indirectly accepted by the parent generation, due to a history of migration and refugee status. The core of such transformations involves the political mobilisation of ethnic communities. This contrasts with the earlier dominant idea that when you leave your original homeland you are done with political engagement. As Bourdieu (cited in Jenkins, 2013: 93) and Amartya Sen (2015: Xii) suggest, this requires the pursuit of hybridity, multiplicity and plurality through an emphasis on self-realisation and justice. This also depends on the decisions and activities of transnational ethnic communities like the Somalis trying to simultaneously adjust to multiple locations.

Conceptual clarification

The concept of a 'nation' refers to a community of people who share some linguistic, cultural and historical experiences and memories. People normally adjust into this particular national belonging, which is often designated. Numerous scholars have dealt with the issue of nationhood. Some consider it a primordial social phenomenon, while others describe nationhood as a continuing process of reflection, reinvention and recreation undertaken by diverse societies. Under such processes, people continuously form and shape whatever type of nation they imagine and want to be a part of. Then they may consider moving to the second stage, which could be referred to as the statehood level, incorporating more or less formalised routines and structures. The statehood phenomenon, at least in its Westphalian form, is a product of comparatively recent history. Max Weber referred the state as a 'political community' (Weber, 2013: 160). The state concept deals with the formal structuring and organisation of human, social and cultural life. It is here that we have the demand for systems, particularly the attainment of a neutrally functioning bureaucracy and a hierarchical form of social, cultural, political and economic organisation. Obviously, the nation also imposes and projects various forms of hierarchy and organisation, but it is primarily state structures that aim to operate above the nation. This is often the case in the process of making sense of the propagation and application of authority, whether it is centralised or decentralised. The construction of state formations that most of the counties of the world are expected to live up to– with the imposition of hierarchical and bureaucratic structures– is mainly a European invention that, through colonisation and global expansion, almost became the global norm in nation- and state-building (Renan, 1996; Anderson, 2006).

It is the framework of pursuing formalised nationhood and statehood that eventually takes us to the third stage, which is the search for transnational connections. Due to successive global, social and political transformations, it is now possible for people in the world to entertain achieving nationhood and statehood beyond national boundaries. People have become mobile and capable of establishing themselves in new destinations within existing nation and state frames. From here, many people imagine and reconstruct their own forms of nationhood that fit neither the current nor the past nationhood frames (Anderson, 2006: 3). On one hand, seeking transnational connections complicates the presumably stable nationhood and statehood mechanisms; while on the other hand, it creatively combines different forms of nationhood and statehood. In a way, therefore, transnational connections represent discontinuity, while it can also project a kind of continuity. It is becoming the norm for people to try to give meaning to their lives through multiple belongings in different nations and states.

In the Somali context, the challenges within the restricted form of nation and state have been dealt with by several classical works in Somali studies, including 'Somalia: Nation in search of state' (Laitin and Samatar, 1982). English language written scholarship on the Horn of Africa– particularly on the Somali peninsula – has perennially characterised Somalia as a nation in search of statehood. The approach presupposes a relatively homogenous and cohesive nation and society with considerable traditional democratic pastoralism (Lewis, 1999: xi): a society that need only proceed into the next developmental stage, namely the bureaucratisation and institutionalisation of innate socio-political tendencies. These top-down paradigms have been challenged by critical scholarship that portrays a complex nation with multiple heterogeneous characteristics and socio-political spaces (Ahmed, 1995: xi; Kusow, 2004). This shift has opened the door for further contestation of parochialisation and efforts to move beyond this paradigm by engaging in comprehensive and critical multi-dimensional reflection on the socio-political as well as the historical formation, invention and possible reinvention of Somali society. In addition, recent scholarship has documented the manifestations of vibrant economic and civic transections (Little, 2003). This happened in the middle of successive traumatising ruptures following the latest global surge of internal and external extremism, piracy and indiscriminate violence.

This book thus aims to depart from nation state-centric analysis, proposing a conceptually transnational socio-political frame of development and statehood. Building on substantive theoretical analysis as well as diverse empirical data collected on the Horn of Africa and beyond covering transnational civic mobility, connections, associations and movements, the book presents several analytical frames and interrelated arguments. It recognises classical scholarship but also aims to complement it by engaging with the social and political fact that today, the Somali nation is also in search of transnational connections. One could argue that the search for transnational connections represents a discontinuity, but it could also imply a form of continuity, with the aim of connecting the past with the present and future.

The chapters in this book, therefore, collectively explore issues of development and transnational connections from different perspectives. This includes when people are involved in the search for justice and power sharing, in pursuit of business entrepreneurship and employment in the Arabian Gulf, contributing to political mobilisation in Scandinavia, making sense of the attempts to fight extremism by external actors and participating in civic engagement through transnational regional educational empowerment.

The classical works in Somali studies presupposed a situation in which people– in this case, Somalis– will transition from nationhood and eventually move toward statehood. This misperception is, in fact, what led to the collapse of the military regime which ruled this Horn of African country in 1991 after more than twenty years in power. The intention of the rivalry of armed groups that replaced the ousted military regime to further continue the centralisation and monopolisation of authority has so far produced no tangible results either. In the meantime, the conditions at both the national and international level have changed, so that we probably need to reimagine new forms of development and nationhood. The intriguing question is why we should often insist on nationhood and statehood as dominant categories for socio-political development. Although this book deals with nation and state, the aim is to reflect the transformations of nationhood and statehood. These are transformations that are already happening–precisely through the dynamics of transnational connections. There is already a debate on the idea of 'transnational nation' among diverse scholars who have been dealing with the subject. However, this is a debate that remains under development. Scholars grabble with the fact that while the world is currently formally divided into nation-states it is gradually becoming routine to operate beyond the nation-state centric logic (Hoffman, 2004: 4).

Transnational communities

Transnational communities can physically reside in a particular region of the world, while engaging in diverse forms of transfers and mobility through transnational communication and interaction. In the process, these communities link to social, political and economic fields, with the potential to generate a multiplicity of transnational capital. Scholars debate the conceptualisation of such transnational frames and networking. While Bourdieu stresses the power relationship and the generation of social capital in the transnational field, others focus on transformative social dimensions of transboundary networking dynamics (Bauböck and Faist, 2010: 112). These complex linkages can be roughly divided into three main activities. First, there are attempts by transnational communities to join the nation and state system. Second, the transnational communities pursue private individual activities and strategies in which they build both formal and informal alliances within a particular location and beyond. Third, transnational communities contribute to the mobilisation of civil society and NGOs with the aim of promoting hostcountry and homeland-oriented projects and processes.

These relationships make transnational communities a complex phenomenon to study, one which requires scrutinising transnational social mechanisms. It also demands the juxtaposition of theoretical approaches dealing with systems, networks, organisations and individuals. Recognising existing transnational complexities, James Ferguson suggests the following proposition:

> ...We are dealing with political entities that may be better conceptualized as below the state but as integral part of a new transnational apparatus of governmentality. This new apparatus does not replace the older system of nation states (which is -let us be clear – far from about to disappear) but overlays it and co-exists with it. In this optic it might make sense to think of the new organizations that have sprung up in recent years not as challengers pressing up against the state from below but as horizontal contemporaries of the organs of the state- sometimes rivals, sometimes servants, sometimes watchdogs, sometimes parasites, but in every case operating on the same level and in the same global space (Ferguson, 2006: 103).

The centrality of the 'transnational' refers to the simultaneity of engagement on multiple levels (local, national and transnational). What brings the transnational to the core of global politics is the emphasis during past decades on identity politics, increasing nationalism and the deterritorialisation brought on by complex globalisation (Scholte, 2000). In this regard, transnational communities challenge traditional ways of conceptualising territoriality and nationhood, as transnational communities engage in multiple processes simultaneously. Meanwhile, it is not only transnational communities that engage multiple transnational efforts; other transnational actors from conventional states and institutions also operate as transnational actors and reach out to transnational communities for mobilisation, power and resource generation. This is therefore a process that takes place at local, national and transnational levels with complex networks and interactions at micro, meso and macro levels.

State-centred Transnationalism

Globalisation brought certain changes to the ways in which scholars discuss the future of states, territories and the interactions of communities within and beyond prescribed institutional and territorial frames. So far, scholars differentiate among three main theoretical propositions. The first is the statist globalist approach that prioritises the centralisation of state institutions. The emphasis rests on state legitimacy and the processes that depart from state procedures, though diminishing, still condition social dynamics and agency. The second is the cosmopolitan globalist approach, which aims to curb global 'cultural imperialism' by focusing on human rights and multiculturalism. The third is the so-called polycentric transnational global approach, stressing new forms of transnational engagement creating transnational public spaces (Williams and Warren, 2013). Nancy Fraser, reflecting on the existence of non-specified and non-particular state- and society-centric transnational public spheres, writes the following:

It is common place to speak of 'transnational public spheres' 'diasporic public spheres' 'Islamic public spheres' and even emerging 'global public sphere'. And such talk has a clear point. A growing body of media studies literature is documenting the existence of discursive arenas that overflow the bounds of both nations and states. Numerous scholars in cultural studies are ingeniously mapping the contours of such arenas and the flows of images and signs through them. The idea of 'transnational public sphere' is intuitively plausible, then, and seems to have purchase on social reality (Fraser in Benhabib et al, 2007: 45).

Keohane and Nye also talk about transnational interconnections in their pioneering work on transnationalism and interdependence. Their analysis mainly refers to state and market mechanisms and discusses concepts such as 'globalism' to describe processes that take place in multiple interdependent locations with multiple actors (Keohane and Nye, 2000). However, their analysis excludes transnational communities. Nonetheless, like other parts of the society, transnational communities occasionally depart from statist institutional frames. Other scholars apply the concept of 'transnational lens' to analyse the dynamics between processes at the micro local level in connection and activities at the transnational macro level (Khagram and Levitt, 2008). The emphasis here rests on socio-political and socio-economic interactions and interdependence.

Limitations of the state-centric approach

Modern political systems in the form of states mainly employ Max Weber's ideal type of bureaucratic and hierarchical authority that supposedly exercises a monopoly of power in designated territorial boundaries. However, there are few countries in the world that live up to this ideal framework. Most countries, particularly the so-called weak, fragile and collapsed states in Africa, Asia and Latin America, better fit the categorisation of 'limited statehood' (Risse, 2013: 4-6). Risse defines 'limited statehood' as follows:

> Limited statehood concerns those parts of the country in which central authorities (governments) lack the ability to implement and enforce rules and decisions in which the legitimate monopoly over the means of violence is lacking, at least temporarily. The ability to enforce rules or to control the means of violence can be restricted along various dimensions: (I) territorial, that is, parts of a country's territorial spaces (2) sectoral, that is, with regard to specific policy areas (3) social, that is, with regard to specific parts of the population and (4) temporal (Risse, 2013: 4-5).

In our world, there is no nation and state that can claim a complete control of current socio-political and cultural processes. Most nations and states operate within the conditions of limited nationhood and statehood (Risse, 2013: 3-5). Then what about the need for systems? Should we just say that we need to go beyond nation and state and thereby ideally pursue what Heidegger calls a 'power-free' state (Dallmayr, 2001)? The problem is that whatever aims people pursue, there is a reproduction of systems corresponding to earlier nationhood and statehood processes, which is often seen as indispensible. This is a form of imaginative restriction and acknowledgment that means we often need to look backward in order to move forward. Instead of referring to the past, perhaps we should look at diverse emerging socio-political forms. To understand this emerging social, political and developmental platform, there is a need for new forms of conceptual exploration supported by concrete empirical explanation.

As we are currently in an era of complicated nationhood and statehood, we should strive to look for a fundamental re-thinking of nation and state. Somalis today are involved in a form of global struggle that one could probably situate within the idea of transnational transformation. This entails not just a reproduction of the Somali nation somewhere in the world, but also an invention and re-invention of alternative models of nationhood. In this regard, it is possible to argue that what went wrong in Somalia in the first place was the imposition of exclusionary models of nationhood and statehood. In that case, we need to move towards a transformative rethinking of nationhood and statehood.

Clearly, attempts to impose colonial structures upon Somalis and others have so far failed, in this case producing not only a disastrous nation and state collapse, but also serious suffering and tragedies over the years in the form of power abuse and oppression by diverse military elites and warlords. The introduction of top-down bureaucracy and militarisation originating mainly from colonial powers failed to ensure reasonable development for Somali society. So far, these systems have only produced brutal dictatorships and devastating civil wars. Similarly, such systems have also produced the backdrop for transnational connections that originally began with a refugee exodus. When the state system in Somalia collapsed in 1991, Somalis tried to return to the pre-colonial era, in which regional enclaves became a refuge from the imploding state and the subsequent civil war. Consequently, increasing number of Somalis– probably pressured by the regional elites and- seem to favour primordial social and political forms in which clan nations assert power in particular regional enclaves. Even when the state was relatively strong under colonial powers and dictatorships, clan structures prevailed. But the clan system in which current Somali elites operate represent a transformed version that colonial powers and dictators have, over the course of decades, systematically politicised and monetised in order to monopolise the structure of the society through the mechanisms of 'divide and rule'. Obviously, development aid from external actors– both military and non-military –maintained elite dominance in the process of building an exclusionary form of nation and state.

Transnational connections, development and beyond

This book tries to connect to the earlier theoretical works in the social sciences on the subject of transnational connections, such as that of Ulf Hannerz (2002) analysing the phenomenon of 'transnational connections'. Similarly, Arjun Appadurai's major work on 'Modernity and at Large, 2005' and his recent publication 'Future as a cultural Fact, 2013' addressed the complexity of transnational connections. Hannerz justifies the application of the term 'transnational connections' rather than 'globalised' or 'internationalized' connections. He considers the term 'globalisation' too broad for cross border activities not containable within the concepts of nation and state. Instead he suggests the term 'transnational', referring to current global connections in 'scale and distribution'. The transnational term can also help us by referring not just to 'international' entities such as 'nations, states and corporates', but rather to 'individuals, groups, movements and business enterprises' (Hannerz, 2002). More significantly, using the term 'connections' entails what Hannerz calls 'looking at the world in terms of interactions, relationships and networks' (Hannerz, 2002). Furthermore, in the past, transnational connections were mainly reserved for the elites, but in recent times, many people find themselves transnationally connected (Hennerz, 2002). With the emerging notion of a 'transnational commons' linking previously separated populations, social and political structures are beginning to relate to each other. In particular, this is happening more rapidly in the economic, environmental and human development domains (Hennerz, 2002)

Transnational connections and attempts to look beyond the state have both enthusiastic supporters and harsh critics.

For instance, Hobsbawn suggests that both the nation and the state might not survive current transnational developments (Hobsbawn, 2012: 101-102). It will eventually be the nation and the state that have to give way to new forms of transnational connections. In contrast, Smith considers the phenomenon of transnational connections as a transitional process. If it has to prove its relevance beyond the pattern of communication and exchange, it will require cultural and national ingredients that can sustain such connections. The reason why such connections will not prevail, Smith argues, is that the connections are 'fundamentally artificial' and sometimes 'indifferent to place and time'. The process, he adds, 'lacks any emotional commitment of what is signified' (Smith 1991: 157-158).

In the end, what drives people– whether focusing on the national or transnational– is the perpetual search for their aspirations and the use of imagination. This might seem to be an individual or group task, but it is also clearly a 'collective practice' that plays a 'vital role in the production of locality' (Appadurai, 2013: 287). Appadurai argues for the continuing reinvention and reconstruction of social and political realities, as modernity remains not only at large but also incomplete. It is here that transnational connections contribute to new forms of collective aspirations and imagination. Within these transnational connections, diverse actions of 'thinking, feeling and acting' are involved in complex processes of 'counting, accounting and recounting' (Appadurai, 2013: 295).

Though transnational connections have expanded in scale and scope in recent times, this is far from a recent phenomenon. Cultural and social transformations take place through trade, geographic exploration and in the context of changing environmental conditions. In his recent comprehensive study of the historical and current geo-strategic importance of the Indian Ocean and monsoon climate that for centuries transnationally linked the countries around the Indian Ocean, including Somalia, Alpers writes the following:

> The Indian Ocean is characterized by many... uneven distributions. To take one the desert regions in the Horn of Africa and greater Arabia- the latter rich in dates and pearls- but poor in wood- are flanked by the savannah and forested regions of East Africa and Western India both of which have abundant supplies of wood- as well as many other desirable goods for exchange, such as ivory from Africa and cotton textiles from India. Similarly the great attraction of insular South East Asia was its precious spices- while China at the far reaches of the Indian Ocean commercial system- was a major source of silk textiles and other luxury goods. The historical development of these commercial exchanges brought with them in their various cultural transformations (Alpers, 2014: 10-11).

The concept of development

Another important dimension this book addresses is the concept of development. Here we need to think of the transformation emanating from transnational connections not only as a supplement to the process of aiming beyond nation and state, but also as an integrated part of the dynamics of development. This is probably the main challenge the world is currently confronting. This concerns not only what diverse transnational communities are doing with regard to the contribution to multiple places, but also the specific contributions to the nations and states such communities aim to adjust. This is obviously a developmental challenge, involving the dynamics of development and nationhood and the question of how a nation develops. For instance, we currently have in the mainstream literature a discourse that distinguishes developing nations and states from underdeveloped ones. In this regard, numerous global indexes often show that a country like Somalia is almost always at bottom of this hierarchy, while Scandinavian countries often occupy the top. These indices measure everything from health to economic conditions and even happiness. Though such measurements rely on some facts, they do not capture the whole story of development. These measurements underestimate the sense of belonging people feel both to the so-called developed and underdeveloped places of the world. With such one-dimensional surveys, we are therefore talking about the classification of people and not necessarily the self-identification of people. The division between developed and underdeveloped therefore represents a problematic division. The fact that a particular country is economically deprived or lacking in material well-being does not mean that this country is underdeveloped by some other criteria. We therefore need to think of development as a global challenge and a multidimensional process involving both material and non-material well-being. We can instead refer to the concept of integral development – necessary for better livelihood and well-being in all societies (Giri, 2000). In the mainstream, we see standardisation of development indicators, suggesting that there is just one way of doing development. For instance, Fukuyama suggests that the global challenge today is how to move from a situation like that of Somalia and Nigeria and towards that of Scandinavia. So Fukuyama implies that there is no need to learn from Africa. We can argue that transnational communities practicing transnational connections are part of a global transformation that challenges this Fukuyama-proposed static, linear development. Such transnational communities and the dynamics and transnational connections with which they are involved are not aiming to move from A to Z in a linear way. Most of the communities in Europe, China, the Middle East and Africa aim to pursue dignified transnational connections. Unlike Fukuyama's well-known thesis on "the end of history", for transnational communities, development remains an unfinished project. Development is therefore not just static, but the result of the dynamics of an ongoing process that shapes and reshapes development. What we now know is that people scattered around the world are involved in different forms of transnational actions and connections in which people combine material and non-material opportunities for development.

One of the cases presented in the book discusses the link between regionalisation and development. The process of regionalisation is itself also a form transnational connection. With Amoud University, when the state collapsed, the civic educated groups and elders came together to construct space for education that could take the community beyond the civil war Eventually the initiative provided higher education not only for young people but also to the region and to the wider transnational communities as a whole.

CHAPTER ONE

The justice of improving Security and confronting Poverty: The role of Transnational NGOs and Communities

Introduction: From traditionalism to transnationalism

The Somali case with its contemporary complexities of poverty and insecurity attests to a perpetual underdevelopment with colonial and post-colonial origin and negligence. However, over the past two decades competing actors on various forms of transnationalism asserted certain influences at meso and micro levels. The difference somewhat lies that colonial and post-colonial structures applied top down modernization tendencies to centralize socio-political and economic life. While transnationalism actors ideally aim at decentralizing and diversifying with bottom up more inclusive approaches in addressing poverty and insecurity. Finally in order to properly address transitional justice and consolidate social stability, the chapter suggests the combination of some sort of collective macro state formation with substantial space for the gradual consolidating and vibrant transnationalism. The biggest challenge to such strategy comes from the lack of formal transnational "public sphere". Although globalization brought significant practical changes, most societies remain reticent to exploring beyond the traditional macro national sphere.

This chapter defines justice as a concept closely related to the dynamics of security and poverty. The first section presents theoretical perspectives linking poverty and security to development in general and justice in particular. For instance Amartya Sen who supplements the Weberian state and power centric model with the need to address security and poverty from non- bureaucratic organizational approach but also from a civic, social and human interactionism approach. Subsequent sections discuss empirical processes of security and poverty transformations in Somalia during which socio-political structures shifted from traditionalism to more complex colonial and post-colonial structures. The chapter further analyses the current dynamics of power and justice. The final parts of the chapter explore post-collapse and security challenges by looking at transnational civic oriented actors and their contribution to development. More recently the conditions of statelessness forced transnational NGOs and transnational communities to deal with challenges emanating from security and poverty related challenges.

Perspectives linking poverty and insecurity

Amartya Sen connects the prevalence of injustice with poverty. The Nobel laureate does not directly advocate for the universal idealistic eradication of injustice and poverty; two major human development obstacles that for him remain inseparable. Instead he reiterates the need for concrete steps to reduce poverty and insecurity with the aim to improving human dignity and coexistence. Such concrete steps will help us, he proposes, addressing human needs and capabilities in the long term while enabling us to overcome structural social injustice. We can, for instance, start with feeding, rescuing, caring, vaccinating and educating people before undertaking any other social endeavors. Hence focus rests on the realization of justice in real life situations and the message is to implement justice practically and gradually instead of rhetorically engaging imaginary or revolutionary justice discourses (Sen, 2000).

For scholars like Amartya Sen distributing wealth from richer constituents of the society to the lesser privileged components is not enough. Such action should be accompanied by the moral responsibility of giving people capabilities and opportunities so they become engaged citizens that can participate and contribute to "social activities with self-respect and conscience" (Sen, 1991; 1999; 2009). Clearly poverty is not just to suffer from economic deprivation but also that food scarcity and hunger undermines the independency, integrity and dignity of the concerned people. Similarly the combination of insecurity and poverty compromises people's overall capabilities to actively participate in the society (Nussbaum, 2011).

Discussing the link between identity, poverty and violence Amartya Sen suggests that we approach such relationship in tow way:

> One approach concentrates on the culture of societies, and the other on the political economy of poverty and inequality in which the recurrence of violent crime…. [is prevalent]… in countries with much poverty and inequality. [The second approach is that] Poverty and inequality are importantly linked to violence, but must be seen together with divisions between factors such as nationality, culture and religion ….the coupling between cultural identities and poverty increases the significance of inequality and may contribute to violence (Sen, 2008).

Thus the human welfare centric conceptualization of justice contradicts the often proclaimed state centered Weberian approach of linking justice with the consolidation of state apparatus and the monopolization of violence (Weber cited in Poulantzas, 2000: 80). The Somali case, more than others, illustrates the direct link between extreme poverty and insecurity. The Horn of African nation is one of the worlds' poorest and at the same time among the most insecure countries in the world. While religious and cultural differences had, until recently, lesser significant it is mainly the management of the political economy in the society that is the main cause for the excessive violence and poverty. Because of the past and the present gross mismanagement by the dominating political systems and leadership in not fostering human capabilities people eventually failed to perform, participate and contribute positively to the society.

Social movements at the grass root and civil society level represent a critical platform to ensure a proper social justice (Smith, 2001). Such associations not just articulate broad social justice, but also consolidate democracy and transparency by defending ordinary people from dictatorships. In accordance with this trend transnational NGOs and transnational communities ensure people attaining social respect while pressuring and convincing states and macro institutions to refrain from violating basic human freedoms. Their main goal is the appropriation of state order with an expanded social dimension. If states comply with such demands justice parameters shift beyond enforcing laws and security procedures with the inclusion and prioritization of rudimentary welfare for most people.

The transformation of the justice system

For centuries Somalis practiced a mixture of customary law (*xeer*) and Islamic justice (*Sharia*). Under such systems traditional elders and the religious figures (*ulama*) played significant socio-political, juridical and cultural role in structuring and maintaining order in the society. However the traditional systems confronted challenges when exposed to complicated urban environments in which many traditional leaders fail to grasp the stream of unfamiliar conditions. Furthermore colonialism, equipped with western inspired modernization initiatives, demonstratively disrupted the social justice pattern in e.g. declassifying the indigenous socio-cultural structure with emphasis on the dynamics of organization, the overall socialization and rural-urban relations.

One of the most notorious political and juridical confrontations between the two opposing systems, respectively represented by a Somali traditional religious leader on one hand and the colonial administrations particularly the British on the other, occurred in the port of Barbara in the 19th century Martin (2003: 180). The Somali Sheikh, Sayyid Mohamed Abdullah Hassan, resisted the British colonial hegemony and legal system unilaterally trying to impose order in Somali territories. The Mullah, as well as many other Somalis, considered subordination and loyalty to the colonial administration, its security and tax collection instructions, as unjust. They demanded the British ought to pay tax by entering the country unapproved. The resistance movements countered the colonial intrusion with practical traditional religious reasoning as antithetical to western modernization. Colonialists believed they promoted "global justice" by rescuing underdeveloped people from perpetual backwardness (Njoh, 2006: 3).

Sayyid Mohamed at the time unknown returned from extended pilgrimage to Mecca and on arrival clashed with British authorities who imposed Somalis a western style formal border control with taxation and bureaucratic registration. Post-colonial structures whether civilian or military uncritically internalized the modernization tendencies resting on the idea that justice and equality thrives under linear modern developmental strategies. Nonetheless with the collapse of the military regime it was obvious that injustice had long prevailed as Somalia sank into a disastrous underdevelopment path with deeply fragmented impoverished society (Elmi and Barise, 2006). According to one of founding scholars of Somali studies, Lee Cassanneli this was not restricted to economic and political impoverishment but an ingrained intellectual fragmentation where the western approach is the most hegemonic. He proposed the diversification of Somali studies intellectual capacity to include the Islamic and indigenous civilizational heritage:

> "[Somalis have] three distinct traditions of intellectual production in Somalia: the Western secular tradition, the Islamic religious tradition, and the indigenous Somali poetic tradition. Historians who seek to reconstruct Somalia's past have found valuable knowledge in the products of each of these traditions, and analysts of contemporary Somalia have argued that Somalis must draw on the wisdom and experience of all three if they hope to escape from their current national crisis. Unfortunately, most scholars of Somali Studies (myself included) draw their assumptions, pursue evidence, and conduct their research from within only one, or at most two, of these intellectual traditions. As a consequence, our understanding of Somalia has been limited by the fragmentation of knowledge as it is produced, transmitted, and received by successive generations of Somali Studies students and scholars" (Cassanneli, 2009).

The colonial forces strongly believed the implementation of western style justice in a system of loyalty for monetary exchange among loyal clans and privileged social classes. For Amartya Sen colonialism exercises social, political, legal and economic domination that undermines any alternative whether reasonable or creative approach to improve societal conditions (Sen, 2009). Mahmood Mamdani commends that colonialism not just divides and rules but actually defines, meaning classifying societies and communities, in exerting total rule through indirect cultural control mechanisms (Mamdani, 2012: 44). This eventually results macro-centered state monopolization of justice. Even though the judiciary system claims neutrality and independence, it mainly serves for the legislative and executive structures. Thus colonial approaches on justice ignored, undermined or distorted pre-existing justice systems (Muiu, 2011). On their part, post-colonial regimes continued and maintained the militarization and the modernization of the justice system. For instance the military regime, similar to many other developing countries, though welcoming transnational NGO resources opposed people forming formal local NGOs (Bratton, 1989). Instead of taking transitional justice seriously, existing mechanisms prevailed in the process ignoring past injustices.

Pre-colonial Somalia and justice

In pre-colonial Somalia traditional elders in close cooperation with religious figures locally dealt with economic and security challenges in maintaining order in the community. Such traditional figures mastered traditional forms of customary mediation and regulation mechanisms (Menkhaus, 2000: 182). More significantly communities produced their own food locally as well as other valuable goods vital for their daily livelihood (Kundnani, 2007: 36). They occasionally exchanged locally produced goods with imported goods as monetary system was not fully introduced preventing unnecessary commoditization with higher volumes and lesser differentiation. In this regard Somalis not just fed themselves locally but also managed daily security and justice predicaments with reference to traditional institutions. For instance Mazrui argues that due to the colonial subordination, Africans suffer from "self-contempt" and calls for "a return to traditional values" meaning traditional "community generosity in social justice and collective responsibility" ((Mazrui, 1978: 16). Similarly one of Somalia's legendary literary icons Mohamed Ibrahim Warsame "Hadraawi" recently pronounced colonialism as the most historically destructive when it comes to political, socio-cultural and economic discontinuity of the Horn of African nation. In a community meeting in Scandinavia, the poet suggested the following:

> Somalis use to be satisfied with their local simple life before they were transformed by external forces. They use to drink milk two times; in the

early morning and then in the evening...that was it. Then we saw the *hunguri* "greediness" where people demanded breakfast, lunch and dinner and more than that.... Consumption became the key word. When for instance a colonialist came to the country [Somalia] he relaxes in a chair outside his house or office and after eating a meal begins to smoke and drink alcohol. This was often done in front of the Somali cook and boy (servant) and other Somali spectators. The colonialist could consume privately but wanted the Somalis to witness and learn. Many of them imitated and tested and became *afdable* "smokers" and *sakhraan* "alcoholics". From here the degeneration of the society began (Hadraawi, in a statement at community gathering in Aarhus, Denmark, 23.03.2013) *See more on Hadraawi and other scholars' recent visit to Denmark the following link* http://www.copenhagensomaliseminar.net/).

According to Hadraawi colonialism disrupted the straight forward traditional pattern to deal with poverty subsequently unleashing grave socio-economic and security implications. With regard to the structural transformation, the urban concentrated colonial structures started recruiting young men for the maintenance of the emerging security apparatus (Harowitz, 1985: 448). The process impacted the balance of power as communities began losing substantial number of the youth who represent the backbone of the economy. For the youth serving the colonial system in large numbers meant the marginalization of local and regional development. At practical administrative and juridical aspect colonial powers similarly undermined the traditional justice conception by introducing modern judges who implemented a mixture of colonial and Somali rulings (Kapteijns, 2004). Before people used to worry about droughts and young nomadic men battling over local resources, gradually people became concerned with intrusive modern trained forces, imported food, complicated legal frameworks and bureaucracyThe colonial socio-economic relations compromised people's overall ability and integrity by involuntarily and without consultation linking them to international markets (Jones, 2008).

Particularly the Italians took the most offensive position in trying to industrialize food production (Webersik, 2005). Such production was linked to external markets. The expansion made food prices to rise making the locals incapable to remain self-sufficient. Thus the intrusion represented the simultaneous de-localization of accessing food and security. Italians exploited the fertile agricultural regions in the south, while the British dominated the livestock rich regions in the North. This confirms that the colonial enterprise was geo-economic and geostrategic oriented (Gann and Duignan, 1975: 238). Eventually the management of food and security fell into the hands of colonial powers who managed according to their strategic interests. In addition colonial powers had through intense modernization and urbanization in Africa and elsewhere changed pastoral and agricultural practices with serious impact and reduction of the traditionally nutritious locally produced food eventually leading to gross food scarcity and aid dependence (Safa, 2010: 63).

Furthermore intense urbanization following mass migration and the subsequent militarization of the society propagated security deterioration. Somalis like other Africans began to acquire and use modern arms during colonial and post-colonial times. In general modern weaponry "de-ritualized" and demoralized African societies in transforming the logic of power concentration, relation and application (Mazrui, 2004: 10-11). Gun use became widespread not just among the regular forces or for the criminals but also for the average person. The outcome was a more individualistic form of justice detached from the collective traditional one.

In the Somali context both civilian and military regimes addressed society and developmental malfunction with the easier maneuvering of importing alien ideologies such as the uncritical implementation of western multiparty democratic models and attempts to adopt the ideas of scientific socialism (Williams,

2007). Though such shifts temporarily succeeded in mobilizing the masses from the micro towards meso levels, the process eventually failed to ensure long term societal cohesion and sustainability. The core problem was that such ideologies lacked the necessarily required indigenous legitimacy. The formulation of certain macro- institutional strategies in which recurring systematic injustices fostered powerlessness, passivity and dependency nurtured a vicious cycle of resentment in the society. The condition remained the same for the past decades where, due to the decline of justice and trust, few warlords and armed gangs kept almost the entire nation hostage. Therefore the restoration of social justice not by the elites at macro level but also by transnational civic movements at the grass root and middle levels seems indispensable. Otherwise marginalized and excluded segments of the society suffering from socio-political and economic grievances will revolt against injustices committed by privileged social classes. The atrocities in early 1990s in Somalia might reflect brutal vengeance by outsiders who suffered from socio-economic grievances (Ahmed, 2005: X).

The relationship between power and justice

The quest for a "perfect justice" though it seems illusive remains the ultimate goal for a balanced and prosperous humanity. So far, idealistically the process of civic mobilization offers the best option for a society with lesser oppression and lesser citizens suffering from hunger. The bottom up mobilization accommodates ordinary people's struggles and aspirations for justice (Valentini, 2011). Justice and underdevelopment are linked because those with power, if not pressured by civic groups, may fail to address basic human needs. This means power constitutes central to the implementation of justice and injustice. Those in power have the option to either promote justice and fairness or alternatively pursue injustice and unfairness. Legitimate power is often used for improving the wellbeing of citizens leading to the decline of fear from power abuse and subsequent cooperation with ruling institutions. If on the other hand power is centralized and manipulated to undermine the well-being and dignity of citizens, then people will lose respect for this power, withdraw their legitimacy and even seek to take over just to avoid injustice and inhuman treatment.

A visit by Frank Esmann a prominent Danish journalist, who visited Mogadishu in 2012, during the transition from a transitional government to a federal government, illustrates the connection between justice and power struggle. The Danish journalist met and conversed with many people and visited different parts of the city. In a hotel called *Hoteelka nabadda* "peace hotel" he nervously reflects the surroundings in the Somali capital and discusses a "window of opportunity" in search of perpetual peace and reconciliation. He observes the following:

> There are a lot security guards and the person that takes me from the airport is a 26 years old Somali who since childhood was preoccupied with surviving excessive hunger, injustice and lack of security. Inhabitants of the city experience frequent terror activities and countless related crimes. Over the years competing warlords committed serious atrocities here. Rival clans shoot each other wildly, anyone can shoot anytime. A police man who drinks alcohol can do it; even two men fighting over women can spread fear engulfing innocent bystanders…. I visited the beach and the weather was nice and many young people and children enjoyed swimming. Suddenly, our 26 years old security guard and his collogues ordered us to immediately return to the car. We did not feel and see any immediate threat, but in Mogadishu it is the weird 26 years old security guard and his young armed comrades that instruct and have the last word.

Frank Esmann presented a documentary in the Danish Radio on Danish international relations and involvement in developing countries including Somalia and in the process met and discussed with Somali traditional elders and politicians in Mogadishu on issues of power and justice. More about the meetings and the interviews in the following link: http://www.dr.dk/P1/Serier/Brobyggerne/Udsendelsen/20121120133401.htm, (Frank Esmann, 2012).

The security business protecting the Danish journalist, and other foreigners and representatives of international NGOs briefly visiting the volatile country, attest to the prevailing poverty and security predicament. The Somali youth have under the patronage of various ruthless factions in the country suffered over two decades of civil war. The Danish journalist observed the direct relationship between poverty and insecurity through the behavior and eyes of the young Somali security guards. Likewise his encountering with a group of Somali elders had shown him the intricate connection between power and injustice. In a cafeteria across the *hoteelka nabadda* the journalist meets with the development and constitution and reconciliation ministers from the then outgoing Transitional Government. The two ministers inform the Scandinavian journalist the progress they made since assuming power with for instance the formulation of anti-piracy and anti- terror plans and strategies. So far most contacts between Somali authorities and external actors, mainly from those representing of western governments deal with the issues of piracy and terrorism. This overshadows all other concerns Somali officials might have in mind to address. The Danish journalist inquires *"what has the Somalis done for security as it is primarily African troops that now ensure security in the capital?"*. The ministers hesitated as among the Somalis with regard to security it is unclear who is in charge. Certainly the so-called traditional elders play a crucial role. The elder title here does not refer to age seniority but reflects the contribution to the diverse kinship and cliental practicalities. In the prolonged internationally managed so-called reconciliation meetings the elders appointed some of their clan members that in return appointed parliamentarians subsequently electing a president who then nominated a prime minister. As the following stamen suggests, when we talk about elders we are not referring to the classical elders which often enjoyed local community legitimacy:

> Traditional elders (oday dhaqameedyada) use to be settled in the countryside and had in-depth and precise knowledge of the communities that surround them. They were respected and hounourable. But now they are mobile moving around- they live in different hotels and making different kind of deals with many people. They are semi-politicians (Jamaal, interviews, August 2015).

In a meeting with 15 clan elders on a session of a "dialogue on the future", the Danish journalist discovered that the elders expressed their dissatisfaction with the parliamentary members they themselves selected. In a straight forward question, the journalist inquired: *"what does justice mean for you?"* A leader among the elders responds *"We have just emerged from vicious civil wars. It is therefore important that most people who fought in the civil war can see themselves from the new power sharing. For us justice is accessing and sharing power"*. The Danish journalist asks again: *"What do you want to use power for?"* Another elder responds: *"Because in previous governments, we saw those in power abused their power, therefore everybody wants to be represented in the government so they can access power and resources"*. Clearly for war torn Somalis justice and power remains inseparable.

The Somali power centered version of society is obviously far removed from the Heidegger's call for a "power free society" (Dallmayr, 2001). It also confirms that the concept of Justice has multiple definitions and interpretations. One of the conceptualizations emphasizes the improvement and protection of human dignity (Kretzmer et al., 2002). However among scholars how to initiate and achieve such undertaking remains controversial. For instance in modern times the emphasis rested on top down strategies to restructure and mobilize the society and thereby provide alternatives for traditional social structures assumed antithesis to modern social justice and development. The most basic humiliation people could experience is the situation of not been able to protect yourself physically or not having enough food to eat as the result of extreme poverty. In properly functioning democracies and also societies which respect human life, starvation and famines do not occur as social consciousness and solidarity combined with institutional mechanism and "powerful self-cultivation" prevents such tendencies (Giri, 2012: 83).

In Somalia as mentioned earlier security management in the past belonged to the traditional structures often employing customary law *xeer* to solve security problems at the local level. In such structure the elders, which in the past literarily meant those above 40 years and the learned, men with basic knowledge on the Quran and Sunnah, represented and constituted consultative bodies. Together they addressed pressing issues locally. The young men performed significant sociological and psychological role in the process of reclaiming justice. If in case the elders and the learned men fail to reach consensus and find solution, the threat of deploying the power of the youth constituted an option. This was clearly not the last option as peace and reconciliation was the main goal, but it was an indirect factor in the negotiations to find and facilitate solutions. Justice is often served best for those that could support and combine their claims with substantial force. The norm was to overcome any security quandaries with local means and tools. Under certain circumstances leaders often seek solutions in neighboring environments with better learned men or rebuttable elders (Gundel, 2006). The better qualified peaceful neighbors might voluntarily intervene for religious and brotherly reasons or for the rational concerns to avoid spillover effects. Traditional structures dealt with economic challenges and poverty and have also managed security obstacles. For instance, during drought in which fighting over resources were normal, elders held successive consultations to mediate and reach collective agreements that incorporated the immediate concerned of the involved parties. In situations of extreme poverty and disasters people got support from their immediate relations through *xoolo goyn* and other traditional methods of "Wealth sharing" (Sheikh Abdi, 1977). . Islamic principles, through *sadaqa* and *zakat*, of preventing and solving social destitution played a significant role (Bonner, 2005). Despite the limitations of the traditional structure to exclude women, it is locally generated through successive consultations and had in the past enjoyed legitimacy.

The modernization attempts of colonial and post-colonial socio-political and economic structures proved detrimental to the traditional efforts in undermining traditional solutions to poverty and insecurity publicly framed as static and backward. The intense bureaucratization and urbanization of social, political and economic structures required the transformation of societal institutions. Hence following independence modern forms of state and society organization substituted and replaced traditional structures where elites from political parties became the wise men. The state recruited the youth to becoming professional soldiers and police with national state obligations rather than local community connections and priorities. This had nonetheless in the past led to earlier unsuccessful local army mutinies particularly in the North of the country (Adam, 1992). Consequently under modernization, urbanization, the introduction of new forms of labor organization through semi-industrialization replaced traditional ways of solving food security and poverty related issues. In a new poverty alleviation attempts donor supported food security systems with NGOs and missionary activities substituted the traditional methods of intercommunity social capital mobilization. A culture of international gifts, as Somalia's accredited author Nuruddin Farah portrayed in one of his novels, *gifts* emerged making the country increasingly dependent on food aid (Wright, 2002: 569).

Post-collapse security and poverty challenges

Soon after the state collapse in Somalia, the number of actors claiming to stand for the promotion of justice increased both from within the country and from abroad. The major external contributors included international, transnational agencies, NGOs and various Somali established NGOs organized by Somali activists in the country and in Diaspora. By providing humanitarian assistance such as food and education NGOs claimed for advocating justice and the attainment of a dignified life. Initially most transnational agencies and NGOs evacuated due to precarious security condition in early 1990s (Foreign policy Bulletin 1992). Gradually many of returned to join rescue efforts and other humanitarian enterprises. Obviously the stated purpose was to help the suffering Somalis. But the humanitarian agencies consciously or unconsciously contributed to the security challenges that confronted the country. By for instance hiring security guards and bringing money and food in the country transnational NGOs not just factionalize the society and contribute to the vicious power struggle but have also occasionally operated as proxies for multinational interests and companies (Maren, 1986, 2009). As the following statement suggests, NGOs and civil society could be beneficial but sometimes also rather distanced from the communities such organizations claim to represent:

> Members of the civil society and NGOs compile substantial information knowledge as they are able to write reports and evaluations. But most of them focus on funding and proposal writing- making them too much

preoccupied with externally oriented projects (Cabdullaahi, interviews-august 2015).

Eventually the civil war changed from been secular warlord dominated to religious warlords in which groupings claiming religiosity spearheaded the conflict. Sometimes it was difficult to distinguish the different militias and their diverse internal and external sponsors. Meanwhile the south descended deep into violent anarchy, while in the North Somalis partially returned to traditionalism. Overall in recent years the country witnessed increased radicalization despite continuing external interferences (Menkhaus, 2007).

One such intervention took place in 1992 when the US together with a large coalition of 25 nations tried to force their way in to the country to provide food for famine tormented Somalis. The mission provoked serious obstacles when the US sought to impose order over lawless militia warlords. Soon after the withdrawal of the demoralized US and the international system, the more strengthened warlords resumed their strangulation over the society in intimidating and extracting resources from civilians. The religious militias also forcefully collected the so-called *zakat* which they used to arm and strengthen their ranks. Heavily armed warlords clashed over the control of resources especially land and water originally owned by vulnerable farmers in the inter-riverine region (Mukhtar, 1996).

Dealing with poverty and insecurity under stateless condition

In general the state should provide protection and opportunities for its citizens to enjoy a dignified life. In the Somali context of state failure, non-state actors assume this form of decisive social empowerment. Under statelessness condition the strong oppresses the weak due to the absence of mediating basic laws and institutions. According to the Islamic principles, which Somalis adhere, under anarchic security circumstances justice is unattainable. The same applies to periods of extreme economic impoverishment with excessive droughts and famines. This means that in order to ensure some form of justice people need collective structures and institutions. For decades such goals remained elusive and in the transition period people resort to community organized self-defense activities for protection. The challenge herewith lies with the delicacy to balance the personal need for safety with the limits of avoiding transgression. Apparently fear from state authorities is terrible but such structures are necessary in maintaining order and preventing chaos. The biggest challenge under statelessness, as it happened in Somalia, is the privatization and commercialization of armed militias. No-one knows where to get protection from unless one bribes or allies with certain armed hegemonic groups. The immediate concerns and priority for most people is to stay alive. Thus under such statelessness condition no obvious hegemon or sovereign exists consequently making life brutish and short (Hobbes cited in Firebaugh, 2006: 3).

In terms of poverty and food security statelessness creates serious challenges for ordinary people. Obviously the bad security condition fosters severe economic decline and lack of education gradually undermining the organization of productive force and mobility. Subsequently the worsened security condition leads to abject poverty and hunger. People might eventually adjust to existing realities and search for local solutions that could make them stronger to cope with the persistent insecurity. The sustained hardship convinces people to optionally seek a collective security approach. From this endeavor bottom up socio-political structures emerge. Such structures rest on national and transnational civic engagements that advocate for the improvement of human security as well as the economic conditions.

Colonialism replaced the original traditional societal approaches to address security and poverty deficiencies to a top down authoritarian bureaucratic mechanisms. Its core pillars rested on the closer cooperation of foreign countries and the local elites with the centralization of security and economic institutions. This approach contradicted the original traditional conceptualization of security and poverty which delegates substantial responsibility and decision making to the community level. According to the socio-religious tradition of the Somalis protection to avoiding insecurity and poverty is divinely guaranteed unless human greediness and laziness distorts such privileges.

In pre-colonial Somalia empires and city states ensured security at coastal areas while it remained localized in the interior. Later colonial powers came and imposed their preferred security frames. The top down securitization process divided the Somalis into proponents and opponents of the colonial system. So the macro militarization and division of the Somali people in its modern sense represents the quintessential of colonialism. If Somalis in the past had to watch out neighboring clans, under colonialism they added colonial alliances and imported fire arms into the security equation. The most confrontational clans faced genocide due to their fierce opposition to the colonial system, while others temporarily benefited from their colonial affiliation (Barnes, 2007). In essence colonialism expanded the fear of physical violence deep into the indigenous social fabric (Mamdani, 2002: 207). In general under modernization tendencies societies experience significant levels of state violence than that is found in traditional societies (Huntington, 1968: 4).

Post-colonial structures continued the militarization and urbanization of the Somali society as Mogadishu took the central stage in the quest for both nationhood and statehood. As reported in numerous historical narrations among them the accredited Ibn Battuta reports Somalis had limited security and poverty challenges prior to the colonial expansion. The transformation of the administrative apparatus and the economy particularly served for the designated export economy rather than for the producing peasants, although some scholars argue people entered such markets for mainly rational profit gains (Cassanelli, 1982: 112). The experiment impoverished Somalis further due to the creation of macro security apparatus forcing the peasant youth to seek for employment at urban centers (Samatar, 1989: 5). The process significantly affected the earlier productive localized self-sufficient communities. Urbanization had in this regard increased poverty as people gradually produced less and became heavily dependent on foreign imports.

Security in terms of accessing minimum food requirements and avoiding physical aggression to maintain survival remains fundamentally consistent with human existence and justice. In our current world Somalia and Somalis symbolize the quintessence of insecurity and extreme poverty. This human degradation began during colonial times and intensely exacerbated during the military regime and the subsequent state collapse. In the current statelessness void the efforts to improving security and reducing poverty emanates from transnationalized constituents in a highly contested environment.

Under such anarchic condition national and transnational movements and organizations from micro and mezzo levels often navigate between conflict and peace. It is a dual-edged applicable to both positive and negative intent. The current dominant non-state development actors i.e. transnational NGOs and transnational diaspora communities, share certain commonalities. Both components have, for instance, potentials to provide justice for people in Somalia. Nonetheless Diaspora also exerts both positive and negative impacts on the security situation of the country. Transnational communities have through "boomerang" networking in multiple locations performed critical roles in peace and conflict situations (Paffenholz, 2010: 419). Valuable Diaspora contributions include the local regional and national developments including the formation of relatively autonomous regional structures of Puntland and Somaliland (Hagmann and Hoehne, 2008). On the unfortunate side, transnational communities have also increasingly and openly sustained divisive clanism, regionalism and in certain cases of warlordism (Vinci, 2006). Furthermore religious conservatism partially entered the country through Diaspora as former students returning from the Arabian Peninsula and Egypt introduced competing schools and interpretations promoting divisiveness.

On their part transnational NGOs often coordinate with states thereby reflecting the wishes and priorities of their home countries. On one hand NGOs had fairly injected necessary resources into the emergency humanitarian relief. On the other hand some organizations might generate security quandaries. For instance in order to protect their services and personnel, NGOs occasionally employ local warlords thereby indirectly contributing to the oppression. In addition the food and the humanitarian support they bring foster periodical factionalism with further consolidation of the war economy (Stalker, 1998: 123).

Following the Somali state collapse in 1991 influential national and transnational non-state actors emerged and provided relief and rehabilitation for the suffering communities. Although such actors congregate in diverse forms and organizational constellations, we herewith reflect in general terms the efforts of the transnational Diaspora communities and secondly the transnational non-governmental engagement where transnational organizations build coalitions with local NGOs to provide basic needs for vulnerable communities. Many international NGOs activate networks and social infrastructures, often in cooperation with other NGOs that facilitate the development of transnational social movements. The number and range of international NGOs accelerated rapidly from the 1970s onward (Stearns, 2008). Although numerous inadequacies to achieve stated goals exist, the activities of these organizations have partially succeeded. Both transnational NGOs and Diaspora communities perform multiple roles and often operate in complex transnational and sometimes global environments with diverse jurisdictions, nations and territories (Appadurai, 2001: 1-21). Such movements and organizations also share common objectives to provide relief and humanitarian assistance for vulnerable communities. Ironically and particularly during under challenging circumstances, as mentioned earlier NGOs and Diasporas might undermine humanitarian efforts and instead indirectly contribute to insecurity. Occasionally NGOs arm themselves, for mainly security reasons, or let militias to protect them. This involves the transfer of capital to illegal weapon deals that deteriorate existing conflicts among warring militias and the society as a whole (Rutherford, 2008).

The efforts by transnational NGOs

For the purpose to bridge the gap between their home countries and their operational countries, northern transnational NGOs strike a delicate balance between the mission to modernize and the realities on the ground to traditionalize. Their roles reflect different societal approaches and state mechanism shaped by their transnational reach. Major NGOs have, for instance, in recent years embarked in traditionalization activities by closely cooperating and facilitating traditional institutions. In the Somali context, transnational NGOs consider elders as significant partners in the decision making process. In parallel to this they had also provided training and support for women to contribute to peace building activities (El-Gabalawi, 2010).

Though transnational NGOs in the past allied with macro institutions, they were the first to consider reclaiming Somali traditionalism. Both Oxfam and Action Aid have supported pre-colonial traditional indigenous institutions to support the peace processes from a community grass root level (Farah and Lewis, 1993: 6). In contrast macro state formations focus on top down security and poverty solutions. They aim to build institutions and armies that monopolize power and presumably act as neutral. The transnational approach addresses security dilemmas from the bottom up through the mixture of religious and cultural frames. It is the individual and the community that through moral ethics *akhlaaq* take responsibility for the improvement of security that gradually expands to poverty alleviation and related food insecurity issues. So the issue is not to build effective armies working for the state but a responsible community ready to engage mutual dialogue and care.

Transnational NGOs provide an alternative non state approach to improving security and preventing poverty (Helliday, 2001). Globally there are more than 20.000. Their influences have also grown (including consultative and activist roles). The World Bank reports that projects with transnational NGO involvement have grown from 6% 1980- 70% in 2008 (See more at http://theglobaljournal.net/top100NGOs/). The problem is that transnational NGOs claim independence but often rely on funding from state and other macro structures. Such relationship might undermine their legitimacy and accountability particularly affecting their insistence on micro-meso position. In addition the northern-western centric origin of transnational NGOs represents further impediment. This does not however mean they fully comply and blindly follow donor demands. Evidences show that dominant powers have out of frustration in recent years labeled activist organizations as disruptors (Kharas and Rogerson, 2007).

The concerned established states see transnational NGOs applying numerous strategies to mobilize resources across nations. First through the so-called "boomerang pattern/networking" and lobbying approach. Under such activism NGOs pressure governments and multilateral global institutions urging them to improving the conditions of the poor people around the world (Keck and Sikkink, 1998: 129). Similarly through creative real and virtual networks transnational NGOs protest against G8 and G20 summits and expose that dominant states and private companies are unfair to the poor as marginalized peoples lose their land and resources for big companies "Dodging tax" while some governments assist or ignore such oppressive deals (Hertz, 2004). During the latest famine in Somalia which some recent estimates put the perished figure closer to 260.000 people, NGOs and UNICEF representatives link the huge toll to the disregard to NGO calls and "dependence of response to political dynamics" (Straziuso, 2013). In this regard transnational NGOs should in principle be alternative to states but they eventually become supplementary and cooperative due to the strength of state resource mobilization. Nonetheless as Hebba Ezat tells us that transnational movements go beyond modernization, individualism and state centric approaches, creating civil society that attend ordinary people's basic needs (Ezzat, 2005: 40).

The difference between the classical national NGOs and more recent transnational ones is that earlier social movements were preoccupied with power and political resource mobilization. Firstly the new social movements increasingly incorporate their activities with identity and cultural mobilization (Tarrow, 1996). The current transnational NGOs and their movements apply what Tarrow refers to "connective structures" which is: "the link between leaders and followers in the different sectors of the movement sector" (Tarrow, 1994: 124). Secondly organizations deploy "franchising" methods in opening affiliated branches and offices in diverse countries (Tarrow, 1996). Thirdly transnational NGOs often work as corporate watch mechanism in monitoring global hegemony and incidents of inequalities. Scholars in this regard differentiate transnational NGOs as those that are "watch dogs" such as Green Peace and Amnesty International and there are those that are "working dogs" (Forman cited in Ahmed and Potter, 2006: 81). Transnational and national NGOs, operating as "watch dogs" contributed to a 'bottom-up' legal empowerment and confidence building as well as the dissemination and coordination with community-based justice initiatives.

The efforts by transnational communities

The second form of transnationalism development comes from transnational communities such as the global Somali Diaspora that might have rescued Somalia and Somalis by remitting, investing and empowering. "It is---difficult to differentiate a diaspora from the economic and political migration of a people stemming from a socially segmented society and comprising notable differences of identity. The recent character of migration (since 1957) and the segmented type of society constitute obstacles to the recognition of a real diaspora. To take better account of these phenomena, researchers such as Vertovec, 1999 and Kastoryano, 2000) have suggested the concept of transnational community" (Bauböck and Faist, 2010: 42). With regard there are estimates of about two million Somalis in the Diaspora that could be considered both as a Diaspora and transnational community. This was a kind of parallel and possibly overlapping process with the transnational NGO efforts. Diaspora also plays a central role in restructuring the Somali national and state identity as they contribute to the different aspects of national reconstitution. Unlike the first group of organizations this was more at grass root level but there are emerging Diaspora NGOs and formal institutions including the consolidation of Somali state as well as the creation of Diaspora organizations that support and advocate for justice, poverty alleviation, education, women empowerment and general progress in Somalia.

Diasporas original flee from insecurity and poverty is reflected on their engagement on the issues of security and poverty in the country that has also given them to take a leading role in the reconstitution of the Somali state (Farah, 2012: 116). Somalis flee from injustice and poverty and this forces them to act and engage through cross border citizenship activities. Migration is an integrated part of human life. We migrate to survive and maintain a dignified life. Somalis fled from *fitnah* (widespread intolerance and violence), poverty, exclusion, and injustice. Somalis have been migrating since ancient times and had over time established global Diaspora communities. The main reason for their original migration had to do with insufficient livelihood evolving injustice and insecurity. In recent years the seemingly eternal civil strife, uncertainty over the fear over the future and the risk of poverty forced many, particularly the youth often trapped between tapped between unscrupulous human traffickers and the possibility of drowning into the high seas in search of tolerable and decent life opportunities in wealthier parts of the world.

> For us, Diaspora is freedom, development, meeting with other people, opportunity to learn and interact with other nations. We left from our country for two main reasons. The poverty of the region where we are from and the security problems due to civil wars and qabiilsm, we could

not live there. We also want to get education (Interviews with Abdulrahman, Denmark, 2009).

Transnational Diaspora communities' multiple roles complicate its diverse developmental agency. Originally Diaspora itself is the victim of security and poverty problems in the homeland. Significant portion of the Somali Diaspora constitute refugees and dependents that fled their homeland following persecution or the general freedom and economic deterioration under military rule. Many others joined after the collapse of the regime, fleeing from extreme civil war generated perpetual poverty and insecurity. Therefore, Somali Diaspora continues to involve and contribute to homeland developments. Most feel guilty and express willingness to sharing privileges acquired in host countries with the distressed relatives back home. Others involve for socio-status and economic motives. The Diaspora contribution is not just restricted to economic and humanitarian matters but also involves mobilization initiatives and politics. Such multiple homeland involvements bestow Diaspora members certain socio-cultural capital. For instance in returning to the homeland, homeland Somalis often receive Diaspora returnees as heroes, sometimes more appreciated and respected than the local leaders.

> When you return, people in the homeland will welcome you better than their rulers and local chiefs (Interview with Mohamud, Denmark: 2009).

As remittance is often deducted from Diaspora's limited income its continuation might negatively impact on Diaspora's wellbeing in the host country, established Diasporas aim at beyond remittance contribution. Hence, Diaspora members consider the replacement of the monthly monetary remittance:

> We are trying to help Somalia in a way where they can overcome poverty. We for example invest small projects for about 2000 USD. In this way we

will replace dependence on remittance (Interview with Mulki, Denmark: 2010).

Mulki, a 39 year-old Somali lady in Denmark, married and has several children also remits to the homeland. Together with other Somali women in a Somali women association in Denmark they intend to change the monthly remittance to Somalia to a long term strategy of empowering women and children in the homeland. Mulki and the other ladies in the organization believe that people in Somalia, particularly women, should receive micro-credits of about 2000 USD to make them independent in the long run. Diaspora has through such initiatives reduced household poverty (Adams and Page, 2005).

The emerging partnership between transnational NGOs and Diaspora communities could be institutionalized while maintaining some kind of local ownership in the development process (Mezzetti et al., 2010). For instance the authorities of Finland created certain platforms that facilitate coordinated engagement between the formal structures and transnational NGOs and Diaspora communities that contribute to development in the homeland. NGOs funded by intergovernmental and multilateral agencies in developmental projects such as MIDA and QUEST brought local authorities, health professionals from the Diaspora and other transnational expertise to jointly promote health care initiatives (Weis, 2009). The position of journalist NGOs such as international Journalists without borders that condemned the serial killing of Somali journalists, the recent Human Rights Watch report as well the NGO and Diaspora initiated calls for international fight against rape of women in Somalia illustrate the closer increasing transnational partnership between transnational NGOs and Diaspora communities. NGOs often positioned themselves as supplementary or contradictory to the state policies on security and poverty alleviation. In the case of stateless Somalia such organizations expand to the civic level both nationally and transnationally and contribute to formation and the management of nation and state building processes.

Following the famine in Somalia in 2011 NGOs provided the innovative "cash for poor people" aid designed for the suffering communities in different parts of the country. The system helped many victims but also had side effects in the form of inflation, resource diversion to extremists, and in certain extent failure to reach the most vulnerable due to accessibility challenges (Ali and Gelsdorf, 2012). The main obstacle was that NGOs confronted security obstacles. On one side the US authorities prohibited any assistance to areas controlled by what it refers to as terror organizations. On the other extremist organizations welcomed the food aid but not the organizations that provide such aid which they repeatedly accused for covering western espionage. The survival of the strongest and the suffering of mostly minorities, women and children, prove that famine and insecurity is linked to injustice and asymmetric power relations in the society. Despite significant obstacles, networking and collaboration between local NGOs, transnational NGOs and Diaspora have over the years resisted extremist organizations and managed to provide needed food in the country's interior (Menkhaus, 2012). In addition Somali Diaspora is among the first to respond to humanitarian needs in the homeland (Haan, 2012).

Furthermore in relation to community empowerment and in partnerships with NGOs, privately owned educational institutions in major cities provide classes for formal judicial education. One of the well-known transnational NGOs, the Netherland based NOVIB supports local human rights Somali NGOs to document human rights abuses. The organization offers country-wide training on investigation, report writing, lobbying and the creation of archives. Similarly a local NGO called *Haqsoor* has also been established to monitor and form a community policing initiatives through which local elders will have a formalized relationship with public authorities. In another context resource groups established civic institutions such as *madani* in Hawatako, community-driven initiative, based on Somali *xeer*, wherein local residents "committed themselves to joint neighborhood defense, raised local money and hired an independent militia to protect citizens" (Le Sage, 2005).

Conclusion

Poverty in the form of many people suffering from malnutrition and food scarcity combined with insecurity represent the core humanitarian challenge to development in Somalia. The torment was not the pure invention of the Somalis. Pre-colonial Somalis managed food production and security domestically through mainly the application of traditional mechanisms of strategic planning, wealth sharing and conflict prevention. Colonialism introduced transnational economy and politics that linked the country to colonial centers. European powers brought modernization strategies aiming to transform the society from its conventional course and instead create a society adoptable to socio-political hegemony. Subsequent post-colonial structures whether it was the semi-democratic or their military successors, though rhetorically insisting indigenization and nationalism, in practice proceeded with modernization procedures. These social and political systems failed to develop the society mainly due to colonial and post-colonial cold war geo-political subordination as well as the lack of committed leadership with indigenously formulated policies.

More than two decades of statelessness produced certain forms of transnationalism: state centered transnationalism and civil society centered transnationalism. Transnational NGOs cooperating and building alliances with local civic organizations contributed to relief and humanitarian efforts reducing hunger and violence inflicted on vulnerable communities. Though not fully efficient, such bottom up organizations partially fulfilled emergency relief obligations. We can therefore conclude that Somalia is far from a just society. It is a country in a transition from long term injustices to a process of recognizing the existence of diverse forms of injustices. Today's perpetrators of most violence are adolescents and youth, themselves victims of recurring insecurity and poverty. Therefore any prospective authority must prioritize security and fight poverty. In our current complex globalized world, for Somalia to recover and move forward, Somalis must firstly recognize the need to combine of the international macro state and institutional centric approach with the transnationalism meso and micro levels of civic mobilization. Such collective strategy, in which transnational NGOs and global Diaspora communities play a central role, will address pressing issues from multiple global perspectives. Secondly the ongoing national and regional reconciliation processes ought to include public truth commissions helping Somalis to overcoming grievances in justice in general and transitional justice in particular. Such commissions should also consider atrocities preceding the collapse of the state and even the period before gaining independency. Finally accountability and truth must begin with the authorities, those in power as well as non-state actors such transnational NGOs and Diaspora communities. A prerequisite for any meaningful progress depends on the establishment of legitimate central national state institutions with transnational coordinating capabilities.

CHAPTER TWO

Transnational civil society: Contribution to Development and Security

Introduction

For more than two decades Somalia has lacked nationwide functioning bureaucratic Western inspired state institutions. Under such stateless circumstances, formally and informally organized social groups, have tried to fill the vacuum in providing social, economic, security and political services for the increasingly traumatized and displaced citizens. This has raised a number of relevant questions on the character, the representation, and the ability of Somali civil society groups to prevail under a stateless condition in attempting to promote security and tolerable social condition in a volatile country.

Departing from selected theoretical conceptualizations of the term civil society and supplementing it with empirical developments, this chapter discusses the Somali civil society with emphasis on its entrenched indigenous character and more recently emerging transnational appeal. Furthermore the chapter proposes tentative strategic ideas on how to overcome major societal obstacles that have so far confronted Somali civil society in contributing to security consolidation.

Recently I taught a course to Danish post graduate students on the relationship between state and civil society. In extension I considered introducing the students to the Somali civil society, particularly on how these diverse social groups manage to survive in an almost stateless environment. In the not so distant past (about 150- 200 years ago) the Scandinavian civil society, though not struggling under civil war as the Somali civil society did, similarly functioned under not properly developed state structures. Over time through its bottom up cooperative strategies, Scandinavian civil society became instrumental in the emergence of an inclusive welfare state. This led to an expanded form of public institutions that subsidized, formalized and to a certain extent professionalized most of the earlier largely civil society managed social activities such as feeding, protecting, educating and empowering people.

Finally the chapter theoretically argues that the colonial state, through education and socialization, had left behind corrupt leaders that dominated the first Somali republic and the subsequent military takeover. The militarization of the society divided the Somali people into proponent and opponent contingents, subsequently leading to migration and brain drain. This has prevented the country from exploiting its human capital, paving the way for oblivious warlords to replace the illegitimate military regime that mostly rested on external support from superpowers. Eventually the process culminated into the trans-nationalization of Somali civil society through transnational community formations that initially began in the Middle East and East Africa and more recently expanded globally.

The theoretical assertion is supplemented with empirical observations suggesting that in classical times the Somali civil society followed professional traits rather than regional and genealogical trajectories. It was colonialism that first divided civil society into proponents and opponents in relation to the prevailing system. This cyclical pattern continued until the recent warlordism and anarchy. With the transnationalization of the Somali civil society, through the global transnational community formations together with the emergence of a professionalized Somali civil society in the country, Somalis might balance and combine elements from the pre-colonial past with emerging global opportunities.

Conceptualizing civil society

In Western scholarship the Hegelian perspective on the concept of the civil society dominates the debate. Hegel places civil society groups in an intermediate position between the family and the state. This refers to the meso structures between micro and macro institutions in the society. In general the theoretical debate on civil society focuses on whether the state generates civil society or it is the reverse. Hegel tries to bridge the gap between the individual insistence on autonomy and freedom and the social dimension of insisting conceptual heteronomy. This means that we can try to operate in the natural world autonomously, but in the process we need to refer to the "heteronomously structured society" (Mack, 2001). Hegel argued that societies should overcome poverty and class divisions in trying to provide most citizens with the freedom essential to social organization.

Though Hegel is the main reference for the West, we also need to recognize relevant conceptualization attempts prior to European industrialization. We know oriental thinkers dealt with the tension between civil society and state. For instance Ibn-Khaldun considered civil society significant for the process of civilizational development that requires extensive division of labour and established organizations and legal frameworks. Ibn-Khaldun argues justice among members of the society as essential for civilizational development, otherwise social decline and human deterioration becomes inevitable (Ibn-Khaldun, 1979). In addition Ibn-Khaldun with his empirical epistemological approach helps us to overcome the dichotomies of modernism versus religiosity, and instead calls for a dialogical understanding to overcome the assabiya (semitimental group solidarity) based social development (Zeidi, 2011:20).

Additionally we can supplement the thesis considering civil society as transition with the idea of social society as a social space distinct from the state and the capitalist economy. Tocqueville (1835/1945, 1840/1945) states that such civil society consists of 'voluntary associations' such as 'families, churches, neighbourhoods' and a 'free press'. This is the space Marx conceptualized as space for the productive forces in the society. Calhoun proposes that such space empowers the civil society:

> "Such arguments placed a new emphasis on the social integration of a people, on society as such rather than merely on the aggregation of subjects. In such a view, the state no longer defined the political community directly, for its own legitimacy depended on the acquiescence or even support of an already-existing political community" (Calhoun, 1993: 270–1).

In this regard Habermas's analysis of the public sphere is relevant to comprehension of the relationship between civil society and state institutions. Habermas suggests that the public sphere provides a space for a mutual learning process for competing diverse components of the society and that it will prevent fundamentalism that could threaten the collective wellbeing. He considers the public sphere as an intermediate space between the formal level of policy formulation and regulation (the state or the system world) and the level of private interests (the life world) (Habermas, 1991). Interestingly the public sphere is not immune from state manipulation. In Ataturk's secular Turkey civil society is constructed as an institutionalized public space for modern Western imagination in the process, excluding an expression of Turkish Muslim social imagination (Gole, 1996: 136).

There is, nonetheless, a need to detach civil society not just from the state but also interest groups. The link between the interest groups and civil society is that it is assumed that civil society organization can offer a "short cut" for political parties to find potential candidates and even funding. Eventually the civil society organizations expect support from the candidates they supported when they conquer state mechanism (Katz & Mair, 2012).

The main analytical challenge for the conventional conceptualization of civil society is the inability to distinguish civil society from interest groups. For instance, in the US farmers, women's groups, medical associations, bar associations, etc. are treated as interest groups. While its counterparts in African organized communities are framed as a civil society. Obviously civil society formations are mostly interest groups. Interest and mission remains vital for human survival. Particularly in the neo-liberal pluralist oriented US the focus rests on the specific individual exclusive group interest, while in other parts of the world, emphasis might rest on the idea of collective inclusive interest aggregation.

To overcome the interest trap we could focus on Social capital defined as a private and public good with potential positive and negative externalities (Dasgupta, 2000). A proper positive externality could be moral social codes inscribed into religions requiring the treatment of all humans as equal, not just your immediate relations. Building on Robert Putnam's work, Dasgupta suggests:

> In an early definition, social capital was identified with those "... features of social organisation, such as trust, norms and networks that can improve the efficiency of society by facilitating coordinated actions"

(Putnam et al., 1993: 167). As a characterization this appears beguiling, but it suffers from a weakness: it encourages us to amalgamate strikingly different social capital occur somewhere between the individual and the State: they are conducted within informal institutions. Indeed, social capital is frequently identified with the workings of civil society (Putnam et al., 1993; Putnam 2000). If the externalities are positive, as in the case of making friends (or becoming literate and numerate as a prelude to enjoying advanced communication links), there would typically be an undersupply. There can also be negative externalities in the creation of channels, such as those within groups that are hostile to one another. One would expect an oversupply of them (they are often neighbourhood 'arms' races; Gambetta, 1993). Be they positive or negative, externalities give rise to collective inefficiency. Positive externalities point to an argument for public subsidy, negative ones for investment in such institutions as those whose presence would lower the externalities ('taxing' the corresponding activities would be another possibility) (Dasgupta, 2005).

Civil society seems to emerge from an internal as well as external dialectics continuously shifting from proponents to opposition depending on prevailing circumstances. This confirms that in the society there exist institutionalized social conditions as classics such as Durkheim proposed. Often we also witness repetitive cyclical social relations as Ibn-Khaldun suggested where we move in circular patterns reflecting a rise and decline dialectics. In addition most civil society groups demonstrate hybridity capabilities in socially adapting to the prevailing social conditions while in other situations opposing or remaining proponent of occasionally simultaneous social transformations. This makes civil society diverse and complex, reflecting the social choice and strategic planning of those involved and their ability to mobilize political and structural opportunities as well as framing structures. Clearly in the long term the cyclical pattern of civil society (in the proponent and opposition condition) is not sustainable as civil societies under prolonged conflict such as the Somalis reach a sort of dead end.

In search for alternatives, we first need to replace the cyclical social condition with more progressive cooperative engagement among conflicting civil society groups. Secondly there is a need to transform the core power structures and relations in the society. This could start with the creation of a neutral space, where the diverse civil society groups (at least those working with positive externalities that improve basic social conditions of the society) can meet and exchange their views and ideas for the benefit of the rest of the society. This holds the state maneuvering back into the top of the political society. The paradox is that on one hand we need state institutions to safeguard and ensure a vibrant public space under which civil societies need to operate and develop. While we on the other hand need to remain skeptical to macro state institutions dominating and designing social processes that should in normal circumstances remain bottom up and inclusive. A democratic and more inclusive state would, nonetheless, partially address this dilemma. In return that will demand trust and compromise from civil society groups.

The dynamics of state-civil society relationship	State	Civil society
Sate	State centered approach structuring and manipulating civil society	Partially horizontal relationship between state & civil society. State based its policies on civic engagement concerns
Civil society	Hierarchical relationship between state and civil society, where the state is partially receptive towards civic engagement	Stateless and weak state condition where civil society substitutes the state in providing services Alternatively and global civil society that pay pass the state

The dynamics of state-civil society relationship in Somalia

Competing models for civil society

Fragmentation

Following the modernization of societies, new forms of social, political and economic organization emerge. These are intermediate social organizations that locate between the family and the state. This implies a transition from a particular interest to common interest. Modernization means moving people from badawa to hadara, from mechanical to organic relationships and from gemmenshieft to Gasselshieft. This is the linier development towards more a industrialized, secularized, de-traditionalized society with strong coercive government institutions. The assumption is when the state is fully modernized and consolidated the CS will assimilate. Society shifts from micro level to macro.

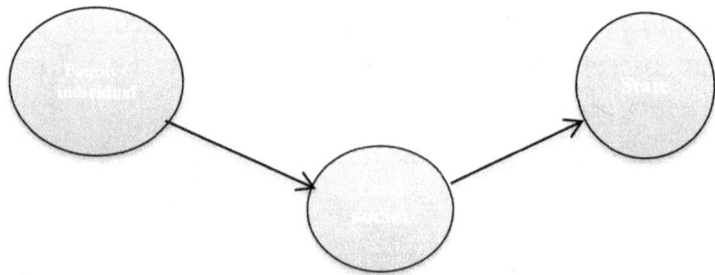

Consolidation/Hegemonization

This is the stage where the state gradually consolidates. It allows the emergence of public life as alternative to private or household-based activities. This happens in the form of non-governmental actors conducting non-coerced activities. We could also characterize this sphere as a public sphere, a site filled with associational life, arenas for public deliberation. It could also be the sphere of self-organization – meso level. This is also a sphere reflecting the bastion of class hegemony, the inevitable coercive and consensual, soft or hard power, the cultural and the hard core politics, the power with persuasion. From this public sphere social movements with emphasis on citizenship expression and articulation of social capital emerge (Putnam, 2001).

Transformation

Critics point to the non-neutrality of the public sphere. It is Eurocentric and state centric and propagates for liberalism, modernization, realism. In addition it is gendered and ethno-centric as it ignores traditions, the kinship networks, the family and the transnational dimensions of human relations and aspirations. Therefore we need non-state-centered transnational global oriented civil society that collectively addresses global inequalities, underdevelopment and injustice. By doing this we will overcome essentialization and predetermined categorization.

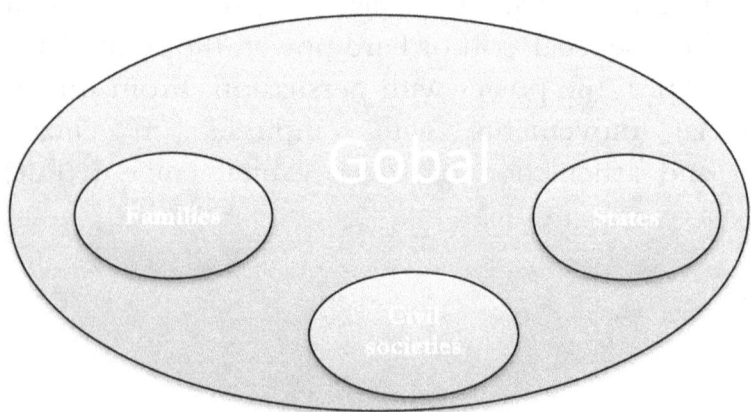

The Somali civil society

If we apply Hagel's approach to the Somali context, the closest we get to civil society would be the warlords. For a while these warlords served as a cushion, indeed a brutal one, between the state and society. Other parts of the Somali civil society are not monolithic. Some are organic to society and serve a real need in diverse communities, while others carry private and personal outfits.

Although the role of civil society, its capacity and scope have increased since 1991, as Professor Mahadallah argues in the exchange I had with him in the following statement, its character was shaped by political developments going back to colonialism. The Somali civil society suffered from colonialism, military dictatorship and continues to do so under the recent multiple external interventions and regional clanism.

> The colonial regimes have actually laid the foundation for Somalia's recent civil society. They had created labor organizations, especially in the civil aviation and transportation industry. There were also a significant number of agricultural groups in different commodities, such as fruits and cotton. Most of these had participated in the anti-colonial struggle. After

independence, they thought (erroneously) that they did not need to protect themselves from their kinsmen leaders. Some also joined the government. That was the beginning of their end. After the overthrow of the civilian regime, the Military Regime finally disbanded them. Later on, the regime brought them back in the form of parastatals. They were cheerleading for the regime. My problem is how to demarcate the line between civil society and interest groups. Are they synonymous? Is interest segregation v interest aggregation a good distinction of them? I know that there are interest groups that try to link with other groups for certain purposes (Mahadallah, April 2012).

The issue of what groups of the society should we include as civil society is rather controversial. We could probably consider Somali warlords as members of the civil society. Actually in the West mafia groups, racist and terrorist networks are considered non-state members of the society that aggregate social capital with negative externalities, thereby being disadvantageous for the overall collective society. The state then tries to reduce their negative impact through information, empowerment, education, and eventually imprisonment etc.

We can roughly divide the development of Somali civil society into five main stages. The first is the pre-modern periods, probably going back thousands of years. Somalis then were divided into socio-professional groups representing biyomaal, baajamaal, muruqmaal and maskax maal social groups. In ancient Somalia, that among others interacted with Chinese and Egyptian civilizations, people's professional characteristics were more important than their genealogical profiling.

The second period refers to the modernization era including the injection of colonialism into the country. Intense struggle between the preservation of a traditional society versus colonial modernization attempts characterized the period. The Somali civil society had the option to either adopt the livelihood presented by colonial powers or oppose imperialism and its cultural, economic and political influence.

Fragmentation that started with the so-called colonial modernization continued until the transnational disintegration during which civil society groups connected to semi-autonomous regions, clans and diasporic interest groups. Strangely the most consistent and the least disjointed civil society groups are merchants that continue to control the market and thereby dominate the society. Similarly women, youth and professional groups play lesser but significant roles. Particularly women groups played a significant role during the struggle for independence, under dictatorship, during the collapse and continue to support and facilitate humanitarian activities in Somalia. It is well known that traditional communities often challenge modernization. The educated elite have in periods contributed to development but have been in recent years, similar to other groups, split into regional and clan groups undermining the emergence of a consistent national project.

During modernization and colonization civil society divided itself into religious and nationalistic camps to counter colonial powers and their missionary programmes. Colonial powers divided the Somali society into traditional and modern components, implicitly referring to for and against the colonial system. Those who embraced the colonial project qualified as modern and civilized components, while those preserving their traditional values, whether religious or customary, reflected backwardness and recalcitrance. Part of the secularized and urbanized society initially supported the colonial system. Colonial urbanization was far from a functional process based on cosmopolitan and civilizational interaction with the outside world. It was rather a distorted urbanization under which colonial administrations recruited clients for auxiliary positions in the colonial machinery such as security personnel, drivers and domestic workers. The process created gaps in the society where people working with the colonial system imitated colonial cultures, while opponents scorned such practice.

Colonialism divided the Somali society. For the Somalis it was not just an issue of opposing foreigners invading your country, but also an issue of resisting enslavement and total subordination under colonial rule. Colonial representatives considered themselves as superhuman and expected people to serve them as their masters. Taking sides with regard to colonial powers had consequences for the mobilized civil society. Opponents of the colonial system risked torture, imprisonment and execution while proponents risked their lives and eventual exile when colonialism ended.

> When colonizers came during colonialism, Somalis became divided into struggling colonial lines. Colonial powers specially the Italians humiliated and enslaved the Somalia. The British also divided the labour so that people from minorities should cook the food and wash clothes. Some of them protested. Some rejected and some accepted. CS was divided into pro and against colonialism. Those who opposed were fighting, using traditional fighting tools such as tooreey. Those who opposed, most were killed. Colonial powers used to rape Somali women. The colonial powers created tension among the Somalis. In their health sector the colonial powers also manipulated as they helped those they want and deprive from those they don't like. During independence, those who supported colonialism fled with them. In Italy most women who fled with the Italians are now seniors and they are suffering. They used to work as spies for colonial powers, particularly for the Italians (Halima, May 2012).

After independence, people expected that Somali independence will bring peace and prosperity. That did not happen and most people were disappointed and longed for better conditions.

> There was a widespread killing and prostitution and suffering resulting from increased urbanization, and elite mismanagement following independence (Ali, May 2012).

At the time, the military was one of the few national institutions not infected by widespread tribalism and corruption. The situation was unbearable for ordinary citizens and politicians increasingly became factionalised across regions and clans. The military took power in a speculative coup after the assassination of the president in 1969. This again led to the division of the society into a pro and against the regime. Since then Somalis have been divided and continue to be so.

> Later, after independent tribalism increased and Somalis confronted each other leading to the military takeover in 1969. From there Somalis were again divided pro or against the military regime. Those that opposed the system did it discretely. Civil society were divided those that "la jaanqaaday" with the system. Production and agriculture started. To opposing forces, a lot mobilization- state mobilization. Now the Somali CS are tired from wars and conflicts (Hassan, May 2012).

The third period introduced authoritarianism during which civil society again found itself divided into pro and against dictatorship. Actually dictatorship continued the oppression began by colonial powers. Colonialism divided the society into traditional and less traditional components, while the authoritarian system complicated that earlier division. Following independence people trained by colonial powers within and outside the country accessed and attained privileges. Actually colonial powers together with the UN observed the transition period leading a form of post-colonial era. Clearly the post-colonial elite became corrupt as expected, leading the military takeover in 1969 that also divided the society into pro revolutionary regime and opponents. The military regime engaged the militarization and through orientation centres polarized society by creating militias (guulwadayaal), widening the gap between the civil society. This resulted in intensive emigration and brain drain as many civic groups left the country for either exile or to join the opposition groups abroad.

The militarization of the diverse African societies mainly came with European colonization as the structures of the colonial military and bureaucratic organization were modeled on British, Italian or French standards, including the rituals of marching and the applied terminology, all becoming Europeanized in "tone" and "style" (Mazrui, 1976). When colonial powers nominally left, the African leaders they trained concentrated on national sovereignty and security and spent the scarce resources on the construction of one party military regimes, leading to dictatorship and economic decline (Bratton, 1989). The colonial transformation of the Somali society is best captured by the following remarks of Abdi Samatar:

> Although pre-colonial pastoralism was not isolated from the mercantile world, the latter had marginal influences over the reproduction of everyday life. But over the last century the new relationships between pastoralists, merchants, and the state have entailed the emergence of different social relations and the demise of communitarianism. …Pastoral Politics The imposition of a state on the old Somali order has also eroded pastoral democratic practices with far-reaching and lethal repercussions. One of the legacies of colonial administrations was the neglect and commercialization of pastoralism and peasant agriculture, and the absence of any vibrant new productive enterprises. In the context of an impoverished economy, small but rapidly growing social groups involved in trading, as well as state employees, came to demand independence in the I 950s, and the Somali Republic emerged from the union of Italian and British Somalilands on I July I 960. The leadership in both the public and private sectors was dominated by a group of Somalis who had little experience of, let alone much attachment to, either livestock and/or peasant agriculture. Moreover, they were overwhelmingly ill-equipped to devise and implement a successful strategy for development. The new regime inherited an anaemic economy, a deepening budgetary deficit, a multi-party political system, a growing urban population largely unhinged from productive labour, and intensifying competition among dominant social groups for resources (Samatar, 1992).

The significance of art and oratory for civil society

Oratory is important in the Somali culture, also in the struggle against colonial powers and the mobilization of the civil society. The best known cases are from the application of poetry by the freedom fighter, Sayid Mohamed Abdulla Hassan, popularly ridiculed by the British Empire as "Mad Mullah". He convinced the Somalis that the Jihad against colonial powers was holy, religious and nationalistic duty. The use of literature and oratory continues in post-independent periods.

> Literature was important in this regard. For instance Sayid (the former president) used poetry and military engagement to fight colonialism. In general literature was significant. During independence Somalis focused on nationalism and people sang and recited nationalistic poetry (Asha, May 20012).

In his book "Literature, clans and the nation state in Somalia", Ali Jimale Ahmed argues that language, literature, myth and symbols are important in our understanding and construction of societies. Language is thus not neutral and spoken in a vacuum. Ahmed suggests that the state is preoccupied with language, myth and symbols to consolidate its grip on power and "oblivious to subtle messages directed at undermining its power base" (Ahmed, 1996: 5).

The fourth stage is the period of state collapse and warlordism, where civil society again suffered and tried to fill the vacuum of state collapse. Here they provided service while bribing the warlords to save their lives. During the collapse civil society in Somalia was organized through civil and non-civil formations (warlords and troublemakers).

During the collapse of the Somali state, most civil society groups either left the country or subordinated their activities under the different warlords competing for resources in the country. A few organizations have nonetheless managed to provide health and education services. The warlords were also divided into secular groups terrorising people and religious groups exploiting their religious positions. Both groups utilized identity and clan premises.

Civil society found itself contributing both to peace and security challenges. Since independence, for instance, transnational communities has been involved in the country's development as they contributed to the struggle for independence and more recently the struggle for power for particularly regional and clan affiliates. On the other hand, civil society often challenged the prevailing system. Artists and public intellectuals, academics and professionals have on numerous occasions contributed to the development of political and economic sectors.

The fifth and final stage is the trans-national stage where civil society through the worldwide transnational links to transnational communities. In an increasingly trans-nationalized complex world civil society tries to adjust with the increase of transnational community contribution and involvement. Civil society confronts the dilemma of wanting to benefit from transnationalization while avoiding yet another "imperial conquest through globalization". This is possible if global civil society is able to reduce the gap between top down global hegemonic power confronted with the new popular bottom up demands for justice and sovereignty (Bourdieu, 1998). In addition transnationalism provides transnational communities with an opportunity to engage and mobilize in multisided network frames to challenge the hegemonic order that often partially succeed in oppressing civic engagement in the homeland (Hepner, 2003). For the Somalis trans-national political organization as well as the hawaala system ensures a dynamic trans-national political, economic and social system linking the homeland to global trans-national locations (Horst, 2004).

The state condition	The character of civil society
Classical city states	Professionalized productive centred civic communities
Colonial state	Colonial linked organized communities (mainly from urban educated) vs. colonial opposing organized communities (traditional religious and cultural communities)
Post-colonial states	Regime linked communities (mainly urban educated) vs. Regimes opposition groups (mainly from urban educated elites and traditional religious communities)
Under collapsed state	Warlord, regional and clan linked transnational communities vs. subordinate professional transnational communities

Beyond the proponent-opponent pattern

Clearly the Somali civil society has been divided since the periods of urbanization and colonization. Now it seems that at least most of the civil society long for peaceful settlement due to prolonged civil war and suffering. Public demonstrations by various social groups together with the literary expression by influential members of the Somali civil society calling for reconciliation and peace attest to this reality.

It is also important to note that international actors such as the international community and neighbouring countries and the AU play a significant role in the security situation of Somalia. Here we also need to remember the transnational communities' involvement that could complicate the Somali civil society and its quest for better security. Transnational communities could be constructive in many ways but they could also be destructive in numerous aspects. The communities' trans-national condition is ostensibly unsettled as they relate to multiple homelands and are not genuinely interested in investing in one homeland. Transnational communities find comfort in the hybridity and transitional context, exploiting opportunities provided by such circumstances. This has, occasionally, created tension as people on the ground accuse transnational communities of "long distance nationalism" by engaging and mobilizing people across continents, while not directly paying the price if things fall part. It is mainly the people in Somalia that will have to carry the burden. Most people with flexible citizenships either return to their host societies or stay in other comfortable countries where they access reasonable security and protection.

Strangely the most vibrant Somali civil society groups congregate in neighbouring countries such as Kenya. This has probably to do with Kenya being a democratic country as well as the East African country hosting major international donor representatives, occasionally subsidizing the civil society engagement in Somalia. The increasing number of shuttling civil society elites between major towns in Somalia and Nairobi attest to this. Obviously people seem concerned for their personal security. At the moment civil society cannot fully operate and prevail in major towns like Mogadishu. The same applies to major towns in the so-called semi-autonomous regions.

Conclusion: Options to overcome the current debacle

Currently, humanitarian, social and political dimensions of civil society engagement, though limited, exist in Somalia. There is nonetheless a clear fragmentation into regional and transnational features. Although with the availability of internet and satellite TVs, an option for coordination exists, it is rather difficult bringing Somali civil society into a common cause. To limit the negative social capital and externalities from destructive groups, Somalis could seek international support. For instance, the Sri

Lanka case in which peace first re-emerged following transnational sanctions targeting funding for rebel groups substantiates the need for coordinated transnational efforts. So the issue is not to bring civil society as a unitary form but to try to encourage and channel resources for positive externalities and if possible also foster bridging dimensions rather than bonding aspects of the Somali civil society, by supporting professional humanitarian associations rather than sectarian or regional groups.

Theoretically the idea of the division of the civil society into pro and against the central power holds for the Somali case. It is nonetheless not clear whether it is the civil society itself that generate such division or if it is a top down mechanism generated by dominant national and international institutions. At least with the emergence of a worldwide Somali transnational communities, there is an opportunity for the Somali transnational communities to have social spaces where they can express, engage and mobilize. The problem is that such unrestricted mobilization could lead to additional disintegration. Most diasporic civil societies are relatively beneficial for their societies, but there has to be some kind of state that could mediate and support transnational community initiatives. Without a state it is very difficult to have space where civil society can flourish. With a state there is also a need to make sure that macro institutions accommodate civil society in a way that at least ensures freedom of expression and organization, allowing people to pursue their interest and share their views and prospects with others.

In conclusion, this chapter suggests that what we need is a transparent civil society among the transnational communities and among ordinary citizens in the country. In addition we should coordinate efforts with host countries to prevent negative externalities. Regionalism together with the prevailing clanism, partially fuelled by subversive transnationalism, has so far fragmented Somali civil society. The reorganization of the Somali civil society through professional, humanitarian and possibly religious, and not extremist, causes might help overcoming such obstacles.

Civil society in Somalia goes back to classical times as professionalized social groups. Colonialism introduced modern fragmentation, paving the way for corrupt authoritarian regimes that fostered brutal warlords, who mastered the brutalization of the society. It is not possible to return to the past, but with the emergence of global transnational communities, Somalis could pursue transnational civic engagement that could potentially combine indigenous social professionalization with transnational civic engagement supporting developmental initiatives. Focus should, for instance, rest on improving education, social, health and economic sectors that create opportunities for communities across the country and beyond.

CHAPTER THREE

Balancing national and transnational networking activities: The case of Amoud University

Introduction

The world's interest in the Horn of Africa and Somalia – particularly in the West – has intensified lately, since the United Kingdom and Turkey organised two successive international conferences on Somalia (Hammond, 2013; Akpinar, 2013). Recently, the international community sponsored a major conference on financial aid for the latest state reconstruction impetus in Somalia. With the launch of the so-called New Deal in Brussels in 2013, participating leaders and governments from the North and South have pledged a substantial funding increase to a five-year recovery plan for the impoverished country (Walker, 2014). This is a top-down trans-state and transnational state-building process, bringing in states, transnational agencies, transnational NGOs and the Arab Gulf to provide the monetary aid, while African countries deliver military manpower in the battlefield. The ambition is to restrain the protracted statelessness, piracy and extremism and redress security deficiencies. At present, the international community recognises the significance of bottom-up civic state-building initiatives, but the overall emphasis is on the reconstruction of a relatively effective state, with centralised bureaucracy and military force, which could eventually monopolise violence and power.

This trend is far from new, as in the classics (e.g., Machiavelli) violence and conflict remain central to nation-state transformations (Vatter, 2013: 68). For Weber, violence remains indispensable to the monopolisation of centralised hierarchical bureaucratic state structures (Anter, 2014: 32). Consequently, scholars disagree about the classification, application and primacy of coercive or consensual measures for nation- and state-building. The issue is whether coercion is the only tool available or, as Gramsci contends, cultural appropriation and discursive public mobilisation can equally produce more cohesive and vibrant societies (Lears, 2002: 324-325). Moreover, it remains unclear whether coercion and violence is an end itself, or if the main goal is the installation of authoritarianism and power consolidation, which does not necessarily emanate from the pure monopoly of violence. Violence could also be the antithesis and possibly the opposite of power (Arendt, 1970: 35).

For Ibn-Khaldun, political violence - though central to state formation - is not a straightforward linear development, but rather a complex process that often follows a cyclical pattern, ironically conceptualised as a civilisational progression from *badawa (rural)* to *hadara (urban)* (Ibn-Khaldun, 1981: 119-120). Under such conflict-invested circumstances, state formation follows an unpredictable pattern in which group solidarity or cohesion (assabiya) leads to state consolidation and dominance through different formative stages. Eventually, the rulers claiming superiority apprehensively witness social deterioration from within and the ultimate crumpling of their system, instigating alternative assabiya and new state formation. Traditional assabiya, composed of a mixture of restrictive conservative social norms in the periphery, empowers rural social constituents to operate more unselfishly and cohesively internally while manifesting a belligerent cultural character towards external adversaries.

Political transformations in Somalia partially conform to the cyclical pattern of violent power struggle. It was mainly disgruntled members of the political elite who eventually emboldened rebels to destroy the oppressive institutions of the central government, such as the army. Their fierce opposition to the then self-obsessed dictatorship led them to recruit and mobilise fellow-clansmen in the periphery, largely through the manipulation of assabiya sentiments. The triumphant rebel movements nonetheless failed to consolidate the initial military gains, due to intrinsic factionalism. More specifically, they remained unsuccessful at introducing and organising a cohesive national authority, not least the monopolisation of violence and the assertion of central power in the country. What followed were two decades of brutal civil wars and successive famines with which Somalia and the world continue to struggle.

This chapter is limited in scope to the proposition of an alternative understanding of the Somali debacle and the continuing attempt to overcome state failure. Contrary to an over-emphasis on the primacy of warlordism and extremism in the process of state formation, we consider the indigenous non-violent micro-centred approach to nation- and state-building more significant. This perspective is in line with earlier research conclusions (Samater, 2008). Drawing ideas from Putnam's conceptualisation (in his book 'Making Democracy Work') that social capital takes decades to achieve (Butnam, 1993), along with Tendler's proposition that communities can acquire and regain social capital in a relatively shorter period of time (Tendler, 1997), Samatar favours Somali-owned, bottom-up civic state-building initiatives, in the long term leading to more accommodating and accountable democratic institutions at the macro level. Empirically, the establishment of civic institutions such as Amoud University (AU) attests to such civic-guided and managed transformational processes (Samatar, 2008). Meanwhile, public institutions, whether privately generated or governmental, confront the prevailing neo-liberal world order's relentless market prioritisation that might undermine public service requirements for the improvement of education and research (Mamdani, 2007). In 'Scholars at the market place', Mamdani argues that the submission and the subordination of higher educational institutions to market mechanisms (capitalism) eventually undermines not just the quality of education and research, but also the capacity of state-building itself. Similarly, with an emphasis on similar linear development, this time at the micro community level, Samatar (2008) postulates that the combination of local market mechanisms with traditional community leadership, cultural capital and other community empowerment mechanisms at the local level can regenerate social capital from the bottom. The assumption is that such local vision eventually contributes to the nationalisation and consolidation of state-building processes at the macro level.

We can therefore contend that with Amoud University, a reverse of the conventional assabiya-focused centre-periphery dialectics occurs. It was the fleeing academia that, due to the civil war, sought refuge in the periphery. In the process, they have, together with local stakeholders, established a vibrant educational institution. From the point of view of classical conceptualisations of nation-building, they should have mobilised assabiya in the periphery to gain political power at the centre. Instead, they opted for the opposite strategy: mobilising local social capital for periphery development. Educational empowerment became not just the means of a higher end but an end itself.

Apart from the consolidation and development of the periphery, due to the global circumstances of connectivity and mobility, institutions such as Amoud University increasingly operate not just within a national framework but also within a complex transnational framework. This trend requires engagement with multiple national and transnational actors, often with diverging interests and priorities.

The current complex transnational environment, with diverse macro institutional formations, does not necessarily follow the traditional pattern of national identity and civic mobilisation. We observe transnational identity formations and civic spheres whose challenge to nation and state boundaries seems obvious (Habermas, 1998). Such complicated structures, though seemingly innovative, might favour the elites and thus not represent a genuine alternative. In addition, in an increasingly globalised world, emphasis rests on territorialised localities with specific transnational processes (Hendry, 2003). The internet creates virtual communities that operate not only in the traditional centre-periphery dialectics but also in more realistic and imagined transnational connections between localities (Constable, 2003). The transnational is not just the local interacting with the global, but also global dominant institutions – such as transnational companies and multinational institutions – consolidating their local interests (Keohane and Nye, 1972; Goldman, 2005; Fergusson, 2006). Consequently, diverse formal and informal social networks generate multiple social, cultural and economic social capitals across multiple social fields (Bourdieu, 1986). The process advances transnational social capital that is not restricted to the nation-state frame, with implications across national and institutional boundaries. Understandably, institutions such as AU initially stressed local consolidation. But more recently, the university contributes to diverse and dynamic transnational networks for non-linear and non-state-centric transitional social capital.

This chapter applies a virtual ethnographic methodology. This includes data collected from the internet: from YouTube and social media pages such as Facebook. In addition, more data comes from direct interviews collected through multi-site fieldwork (2013 and 2014) with informants both at the local level and those that operate at the transnational level. Among them were a group of transnational community members who maintain transnational life and mobility between Denmark and Somalia. The efforts of post-collapse humanitarian and civic approaches by the civic constituent groups in Somali society partially reflect historical continuity, in which communities respond to social decline, moral negligence and oppression by coming together not only to inoculate the population from the spreading anarchy but also to reimagine viable alternatives.

Historical background

The history of pre-colonial, colonial and post-colonial periods attests to the centrality of educational institutions, particularly ulama (scholars), in social, political and economic development. In the past, religious scholars enjoyed greater respect and veneration from society. Though colonial powers aimed to curb their spiritual power in different forms, imperial offices occasionally negotiated with and accommodated their community profiles. In comparison, the current ulama and their institutions are more exposed to westernisation and even globalisation: their incorporation is easier for external powers. The activities of AU ulama and the institution they serve and lead follow two main relational patterns. The first is an informal relationship, while the second is a formal institutional relationship. The university's informal relationship aims at the

Somali-speaking people in the Horn of Africa and beyond, while the formal relationship addresses transnational NGOs and agencies that enter partnerships with the university. Locally, the ulama at AU have begun imagining and creating spaces of hope for the locals and beyond. This includes the promotion of economic and job opportunities for the locals. Eventually this led to the university attracting diverse national and transnational students while fostering diasporic connections. In parallel to this is the political process in which AU balances the political controversies in the country by practicing ambiguity and flexibility. That means that AU refrains from direct involvement in the largely sectarian politics in the country. In recent years, much has changed, as the University has become a significant, if a not dominant, economic power in the region, due to the revenue and human capital it generates. This development has transformed the university's previously subordinate relations with transnational communities and other important actors.

At the second level, which appears more formal and institutionalised, the university maintains good working relationships with transnational agencies, NGOs, agencies, states and others with interest and involvement in the region.

Methodology

Applying different methodologies, scholars have studied emerging transnational dialectics and connections between local communities and transnational institutions and frames in recent years. These include the study of capital investment in local contexts and the resistance from local and transnational NGOs (Tsing, 2005); how transnational communities in the host country impact not just the political elite in the US but also public institutions in their original homeland (Deleno, 2013; Shain, 2000); and local social movements, which utilise transnational social networks and even mobilise across national borders (Cunningham, 2000; Riles 2000; Thayer, 2000).

Studying the transnational dynamics of Amoud University, the research for this chapter applied virtual ethnographic methodology in collecting data from the internet (for instance, YouTube, Facebook and other internet sources). In addition, the chapter uses multi-site fieldwork from interviews with informants both at the local level and those that operate at the transnational level. From 2013 to 2014, the authors interviewed transnational community members who maintain transnational life and mobility between Denmark and Somalia. The methodology of studying and focusing on increasing transnational connections between different places and communities (Fitzgerald 2012; Hannerz, 2003: 206–7; Marcus, 1995: 102) inspired the authors to look at the multiple transnational connections of AU.

The study is limited to AU for the following main reasons. First, the area in which the university is located is a province that, because of the emergence of AU, trans-nationalised within a relatively short period of time. Second, Samatar's writings suggest AU and the activities that surround it could be considered a building block for larger community social capital-building towards statehood and beyond. Such a functioning educational institution is expected to emerge from the centre (a capital or metropolis) and not normally from the periphery. Finally, due to the establishment of AU, the local meets with the transnational in different ways.

This study utilises a social mechanism approach in analysing the character of the relation in these transnational connections, with emphasis on potentially hierarchical and exclusive structures between them.

The pursuit of multiple transnational connections

In recent years, numerous Somali universities have begun to operate in an increasingly transnational environment where transnational actors engage and interact with the universities. This is partially related to the transnational governance of Somalia, a country that has lacked a centralised authority and political system since 1991. Somalia was once under the Ottoman Empire, then under European colonialism, and was since independent under a dictatorship.

Somalia is a country with 'limited statehood', meaning the state – if it ever exists – neither exercises authoritative sovereign power over its territory nor provides services. This explains the influence and importance of interactions with transnational actors, such as transnational NGOs, transnational communities, other universities, UN agencies, philanthropists and other international venues for cooperation.

The case of AU demonstrates that as a result of globalisation, increased mobility and transnational linkages, we need to move beyond the traditional emphasis on the dichotomy of state consolidation and state decline. Both the local and transnational communities, following the decades' long absence of statehood, pursue multiple local and transnational linkages, including the need to create a centralised national state. The efforts at post-collapse human development by civic constituents could be categorized under this transnational frame.

Post collapse humanitarian and civic approaches

The collapse of the Somali state in 1991 and the subsequent escalation and brutality of the civil war resulted in an enormous loss of human life, casualties and prolonged traumatic situations. In some parts of the country, the suffering still continues. The violent conflict also had an impact on the human capital development of this poor Horn of African nation. Following the systematic destruction and looting of educational institutions such as schools and universities, teachers were killed and buildings, equipment and books fell into the hands of warlords and their militia. Remaining individual activists and civic private groups tried to salvage the destroyed higher educational institutions in the country. Their aim was to keep the youth away from the raging violence and the streets, while at the same time envisioning alternative development strategies for the wider community. At the core of this endeavour was a committed leadership (educated elite, scholars or *Ulama*, which is not new in the Somalia context) with cultural capital in terms of education and a cosmopolitan world view. Since ancient times, the Ulama from within the country and Asia (mainly Persia and the Arab Peninsula) have contributed to the emergence of relatively prosperous city states around the Somali coast (Kassim, 1995).

Historical position of the Ulama and education

The history of education in Somalia has progressed from traditional religious-based education to more recent secularised education. The contemporary Ulama and their institutions are more exposed to westernisation and even globalisation. Universities in Somalia, like other institutions of higher learning across the world, negotiate between restrictions imposed by locally determined material conditions and prevailing global geo-political strategies and ideologies. With prolonged formal statelessness, Somali local communities, both secular and religious, have so far demonstrated the capability to manoeuvre under these endogenous and exogenous constraints.

Historically, the modern Somali education system has its roots in Islamic Sufi education, in which diverse Sufi orders provided traditional education for communities. Sayid Mohamed Abdalla Hassan was a leading Somali nationalist whose mobilisation of state-building efforts began with a clash between a sheikh returning from a pilgrimage and the existence of secular education for children in the ancient town of Barbara, then under British colonial rule.

Following the end of the Second World War, the Italian colony in Somalia laid the foundations of a more secular form of higher education in Somalia. The primary aim was to train elites and their relatives. In general, colonial education was elitist: educating and subsidising the children of the elite. Post-colonial structures, particularly the first republic (1960-69), were also more or less the same, as elite groups remained more privileged. This pattern changed when the military took power in 1969. But due to mismanagement and authoritarianism-related governance challenges, the second republic also became elitist-oriented and corrupt, which eventually lead to the collapse of the Somali state.

Universities such as Amoud and Mogadishu represent the oldest and so far most successful universities in Somalia since the collapse of the state in 1991. Currently, thousands of graduates from the two universities pursue careers within the country and beyond. Apart from being the saviours and potential creators of what Harvey described as 'spaces of hope'[1] in providing educational platforms during the civil war, the two higher educational institutions share other characteristics. In their formative years, both universities took residence at former secondary school vicinities. Amoud University took shelter at

---

[1] Such spaces in which people resist dominance and subjugation Harvey called 'spaces of hope' (Harvey, David. 2000. *Spaces of Hope*. Edinburgh: Edinburgh University Press.)

what was formerly Amoud Secondary School, while Mogadishu University moved into the former Mohamud Ahmed Ali Secondary School. Both universities sought to alter the prevailing conditions of civil war and warlordism. Finally, both universities balanced the interests of diverse complementary and conflicting actors, such as transnational communities, UN agencies, NGOs, neighbouring countries, traditional leaders and warring factions, while attending to basic education needs.

The current ulama with local and transnational connections

Academics at AU, particularly the leadership, have not just generated and ensured organisational development; they also innovate. Together with multiple local actors, the leadership managed to engage and cooperate with transnational communities, transnational NGOs, transnational agencies (UN, IMO, etc.) and transnational states (Ethiopia, Kenya and other countries) simultaneously. What is interesting is that such transnational efforts took place without a properly functioning state in Somalia. This is unique, as normally educational institutions not only depend on state subsidies and supervision but also seek transnational partnerships within and through national and state frameworks. For universities like AU, state-building and state power consolidation, though important, is not the immediate focus. Instead, AU fosters transnational linkages in an effort to provide education, hope and development for students and the local and wider regional community.

The cohesive conviction of the leadership eventually led to the university rising from its earlier neglected and subordinate peripheral position. Its approach attracted diverse staff and teachers, mainly composed of returning exiles and refugees from near and far away regions, who fostered a much needed educational and developmental atmosphere. In the process, the educated returnees and the structures they created provided a developmental alternative to prevailing community grievances, inter-clan animosity and traditionalism.

The earliest teachers were refugees from the destroyed Somali capital and from the transnational communities. The dilemma they confronted in the province included clan structures and sentiments to navigate and settle, while carefully moving beyond the dominant forms of community segregation and enclavisation. The main goal of the ulama at AU was to create spaces of hope for the locals and beyond.

Creating spaces of hope

Analysis of the interviews shows that AU has always depended on competent and committed university leadership. Since Amoud University was established in the late 1990s, the university leadership initially undertook a visionary role in calling to the public for progressive institution-building. The primary focus was to serve and stabilise a community that suffered from prolonged civil war. In a recent interview for a Somali TV channel, Professor Suleban explained the process of university establishment:

> When the state collapsed, serious conflicts and destruction happened. Those who suffered most were the youth and their education. If there is the slightest instability, education is suspended – if there is fear, wars and lack of administration then education will suffer. The education will be the first to stop. Even hospitals continue their work as they care for the wounds etc., but education stops. Those at the universities fled abroad, those at the secondary and lower classes could not continue their education – nations with their youth on the street will not gain stability. A minority was fortunate to flee abroad with their parents, but the majority stayed behind. So children on the streets who don't have a place to study are problematic. It was transnational communities that came up with the idea to do something. There are two ways you can cope with youngsters.

> You give them education so they can get jobs later on. Or you give them jobs... The education comes first. We started to start universities not like the West to teach and conduct research – but to bring hope back to the youth, to create a peaceful atmosphere and culture, to return hope to the people – that was the main objective, hope, stability and to get the youth back to schools.

For the professor and the people from the transnational communities and the locals that initially started Amoud University, the aim was not just to do teaching and conduct research. The main goal was to occupy young people and get them off the street by creating a space of hope for them.

Promoting economic and job opportunities for the locals

From the initial creation of hope, the leadership moved on to the creation of jobs and opportunities not only for themselves but also for others, i.e., for the locals and students. The rise of the periphery is clear evidence that the region benefitted from the influx of human capital from the declining and later collapsed centre of the Somali state in the early 1990s. Teachers and staff were made up of older and more experienced academics as well as younger ones recruited both from the transnational communities and among AU graduates.

In addition to having a diverse staff, AU also enrols students of multiple origins. The university therefore fosters proper relationships with students, particularly those who migrated from far away. Among their students include those from the region and those from other countries, mainly in the Arabian Peninsula, but even some from the West.

As an expanding regional educational institution, AU also takes on economic, national and social functions. This makes the university the most powerful force in the region's economy providing development and economic opportunities. From this position, the university enters partnerships with the business sector. This led to the university eventually becoming independent from earlier minor donations, as the university generates and benefits from its own economic activities. This consolidation of economic resources has transformed the university's trajectory from careful navigation through traditionalism and localism towards increased cosmopolitanism and ways of overcoming traditional approaches to development. While the visionary leadership provides guidance and organisational experience, the social diversity and complexity of the academic community strengthens AU as an attractive educational institution.

Fostering transnational connections

Transnational communities play a significant role in the development of the university. This takes place through direct personal involvement in university activities, but also through investment in providing economic resources for the university. AU could be considered a transnational community-generated university, as the founders belong to such communities. Transnational communities remain committed to continuing to initiate minor developmental and humanitarian projects, such as the one with a Danish health project. Much more influential groups include the associations of the Amoud Foundation, based in the USA, and some other Arabian Gulf-based associations. The relationship between transnational communities and AU has changed. Now the university is not dependent on transnational community remittances, thanks to increased enrolment and economic expansion; that is, it depends less on external funding. The university might continue to depend on social remittances, but it seems that transnational communities – particularly those in the Gulf, Africa and beyond

– need the university to empower their own children who are unable to obtain a higher education abroad.

Finally, since the establishment of AU, Borama has attracted migrants for diverse reasons, some for the security and economic development in the region and others who have come in search of education for their families.

Maintaining political ambiguity and flexibility

Political conflict in Somalia is well-known. This reality touches AU, which struggles to avoid direct affiliation with a particular political constituent. AU manages this challenge by differentiating between formal and informal relations. Officially, they seem to link to dominant regional political systems, but unofficially the university asserts a Pan-Somali institutional platform. Similarly, AU fosters relationships with national and transnational NGOs. AU also engages with neighbouring countries, on which it depends not only for students but also for mobility as well as economic and political well-being. At the same time, AU enters cooperative relationships with international agencies and the UN system.

Somalia is generally an NGO-ised country, as many transnational NGOs work in the region, mainly from their Nairobi headquarters in neighbouring Kenya. AU implements projects with NGOs, but in a non-subordinate position to these NGOs. Similarly, the university engages with neighbouring countries like Kenya and Ethiopia, as well as transnational agencies and regional and national universities.

Conclusion

In early 1991, the collapsing Somali authoritarian regime unleashed one of the longest and most devastating civil wars of our time. Warlord factions and their militia brutally killed and maimed hundreds of thousands of people, while internally and externally displacing millions. Among the internally displaced were former scholars (ulama) from Somali National University in Mogadishu. The bewildered and traumatised academics fled to the periphery and, together with local leaders, established provincial universities such as Amoud University (AU). Their attempt to reconstitute society began with limited and less formal social capital connections at the micro level – e.g., cooperating and coordinating with local traditional institutions, the business sector and transnational communities from the Gulf. After more than fifteen years, the university has entered a more expanded direct formalised network with transnational agencies, transnational NGOs and transnational communities, with the aim of consolidating transnational social capital. These efforts at a knowledge-centred, civic micro approach to the reconstruction of a war-torn society differ from the conventional state-centric, top-down security and military approach often viewed as the dominant factor in ending civil wars, including the Somali one. However, there exists another factor in the present situation that, if not equal in importance, is probably more significant. This is the shift from localised national social capital generation to more ambitious transnational social capital connections, in a country that still lacks a sovereign central state, which has elevated the university and its leadership to the core of local-transnational social networking dynamics. The methodologies utilised in this chapter include multi-site virtual data collection and interviews (in 2013 and 2014) with staff and students from AU as well as members of the transnational community that interact with the university, people who often shuttle between the Horn of Africa and Scandinavia for various reasons.

CHAPTER FOUR

Civil society, Transnational Communities and Political discourse

Introduction

Within the past two decades Somalia became synonymous with everything from violence, famine to religious extremism. Somalia is a country with contradictions. On the one hand, it is a country with relatively homogeneous people in terms of language, ethnicity, culture and religion. On the other hand, we see a nation that so far failed to translate the cultural and social relationship to a legitimate functioning political and institutional system.

Contemporary experts of the Somali society underline the significance of the Somali language, especially in Somali proverbs, not only reflecting the essence of culture but also everything about the Somalis. For instance the nation's short histories and proverbs contain not only description and analysis of the society, but also solutions to the numerous challenges facing the country (Kapchitz, 2010). Somalis themselves, as well as the rest of the world, underestimate the Somali's ability to interpret and develop their political culture and society through language and literature. The political and economic elite have for decades ignored or oppressed people's attempt to build their society with linguistic and communicative public engagement based on mutual understanding and respect (Farah & Yusuf, 2003). While some analysts distinguish the elite from the mass, others highlight the clash between rural-urban culture which remains essential for the Somali cultural and political development/underdevelopment (Afrax, 2000 & 2010). Urban-rural relationship, partly exacerbated by various colonial and dictatorship rules, contributed to the Somali people's inability to develop joint socio- political structure.

This article presents and argues for the need to pursue two main interdependent aspects currently vital for the reconstitution of viable state and peace in Somalia. The first is the consolidation of viable civil society fundamental for any state formation. The second is the implementation and application of linguistic approach, particularly by the new leadership, in order to obtain and mobilize public legitimacy. The article further reflects recent development and consolidation of the Somali civil society (since 2012) as some of the people currently occupying the top governmental offices have over years belonged to the civic stratum. The core argument is that the Somali language and the way in which the current leadership deploys that useful medium might determine not just the process of obtaining legitimacy for their immediate projects but also the overall mobilization of increasingly globalized and fragmented Somalis.

Nation, state and language

Alexis de Tocqueville, researching on society and nation building, once stated that language is the strongest and most durable that ties a nation together (De Tocqueville, 1835: 28). Among the Somali scholars Ahmed Samatar was one of the first to study the relationship between language and the state in the modern Somali context. He analysed the contradiction of the so-called scientific socialism the military regime was telling people rhetorically and the realities on the ground (Samatar, 1988). The Somalis have a national language that connects them and constitutes one of the strongest characteristics of been a Somali. In addition due to the significance of poetry in politics, in Somalia language, nationalism and socio-political functions are intricately linked (Mazrui, 1986: 39). But similar to many developing countries, the administrative and the language of education have long been foreign and colonial. For the Somalis mainly the English and the Italian languages have often privileged the urban elite and the educated. Later this asymmetry spilled over the state formation process, the ruling elite and the relationship between citizens and the state (Ahmed, 1996: 103). Consequently after independence civil servant jobs went to those who spoke colonial languages.

The leaders of many countries in post-colonial Africa confronted challenges of national building. On one hand they needed to promote solidary pointing on what people had in common, for instance the suffering under colonialism. On the other they have to differentiate themselves from the colonialists. Many of them felt trapped into the past as they often applied colonial framings and language formulations. This complicated the process of nation and state building. Leaders and State authorities often exercise power through two main dialectical channels. The first constitutes top down coercion approach through more or less direct power implementation by disciplinary structures e.g. the military, police and others. The second approach rests on consensual cultural and linguistic rationalization and interaction between dominant authorities and the wider public constituents (Holub, 1992: 77). This form of interaction mainly takes place at the meso-level with the incorporation of more or less informal socio-political structures. In this regard communicative skills with emphasis on discourse and language management capabilities becomes vital not just for obtaining necessary public support but equally maintaining and consolidating legitimate public authority.

Historically European colonial authorities deployed indiscriminate coercive power against resisting Somalis longing for justice and independence (Poddar et al, 2008). Colonial administrations have also, in certain extent recruited poets, artists and other cultural profiles to counter literary opposition expressions (Lobell & Maucer, 2004). Similarly successive post-colonial authorities, depending on the actual context, combined the coercive and consensual approaches to prevent public disturbances.

The evolution of modern Somali civil society

In Somalia civic fragmentation started with the so-called colonial modernization and have since continued until the transnational disintegration during which civil society groups following the state collapse sought comfort in semi-autonomous regions, clans and Diasporic transnational interest groups. Ironically today merchants and the economic elite represent the most consistent and the least disjointed civil society groups in the country. Business groups continue to organize across region, clan and ideology. Through their more or less legal capital enterprise they hold grip on the society. In lesser extent level women, youth and voluntary organized professional groups also perform substantial roles (Lewis, 2001). Women activists played a significant role during the struggle for independent, the period under dictatorship, during the collapse. More recently they have been facilitating much needed social and humanitarian activities in the country. In contrast most of the educated elite remained fragmented into regional and clan affiliations undermining the potential emergence of cohesive nationwide visionary national project (Mohamoud, 2005:38).

It all began when modernization and embedded colonization experiments divided the Somali civil society into contradictory religious, secular and nationalistic frames. For some Somalis such distinction provided an opportunity to counter colonial powers and their missionary programmes. The colonial division of Somalis between traditional and modern components formalized contradicting proponent and opponent categories in relation to the colonial system (Samatar, 1989: 58). Those who embraced the colonial project qualified as modern and civilized components, while those preserving their traditional values whether religious or customary reflected primitiveness and underdevelopment. Part of the secularized and urbanized initially accommodated the colonialist approach. The colonial led urbanization was, however, far from a cosmopolitan and civilizational interaction and progress. It represented an urban distortion in which colonial administrations recruited clients for auxiliary positions in the colonial machinery as security personal, drivers and domestic workers. The process deepened the societal cleavage of between those working for the system, including the imitation of colonial inspired linguistic and cultural priorities, confronted by the opponents of such non-indigenous practise.

Instead of reducing such divergence, post-colonial elites have worsened the situation and classified civil society into pro and against authoritarianism constellations. Actually the dictatorship largely maintained and continued the oppression began by colonial powers. While colonialism pursued simplistic division of the society into traditional and less traditional components, the authoritarian system further complicated and introduced additional divisive lines. Notwithstanding that following the country's independence people trained by colonial powers within and outside the country accessed and attained privileges.

Actually colonial powers together with the UN observed the transition period leading to a form of post-colonial era. Clearly the post-colonial elite became corrupt as expected providing fertile ground for the military takeover in 1969. The military regime initiated civic-militarization processes through its orientation centres extensively polarizing the society though its militias (guulwadayaal) consisting of urban unemployed and semi-nomads. This had exacerbated intensive out-migration and brain drain as civic minded groups left for either exile or for joining the armed opposition groups abroad.

So the extensive militarization of African societies, including the civic components, came with European colonization through colonial military and bureaucratic organization modelling combined with ritualization of "tone" and "style" (Mazrui, 1976). When colonial powers nominally left, their African successors concentrated on national sovereignty and security and spent the scarce resource to the construction one party military regimes leading to dictatorship and economic decline (Bratton, 1989).

During the state collapse and warlordism Somali civil society suffered while trying to fill the vacuum of state collapse. Civic communities provided service under warlord intimidation and persecution leading to the construction of civil and un-civil formations (warlords and troublemakers). Few organizations have nonetheless managed to provide health and education services. The warlords were also divided as secular groups terrorising people and religious groups exploiting their religious positions. Both groups utilized identity and clan premises. Therefore civil society found itself in both contributing to peace and security challenges.

Then Somalis quite unprepared entered the transnational era under which civil society become globally interlinked transnational communities trying to adjust to the expanded role of transnational communities contribution and involvement in the homeland. This raises the dilemma to benefit from transnationalization while avoiding yet another "imperial conquest through globalization" (Zekmi et al., 2010: 17). This is possible if global civil society manages reducing the gap between top down global hegemonic power confronted with the new popular bottom up demands for justice and sovereignty (Bourdieu, 1998). In addition transnationalism dimension provides transnational communities with an opportunity to engage and mobilize in multi-sited network frames to challenge the hegemonic order that often partially succeed to oppress civic engagement in the homeland (Hepner, 2003). For the Somalis transnational political organization as well as the hawaala system ensures a dynamic transnational political, economic and social system linking the homeland to global transnational locations (Horst, 2004).

Somalis long for an inclusive world order

Strong states have always dominated world affairs, while weaker states often exercise little or no influence. Although no obvious jungle law prevails, in these years a desirable situation with a clear and coherent international order does not exist. For most of the past century, humanity endured under a West versus East international balance of power with mutual tension and mistrust. The two dominant global powers, the U.S. and the Soviet Union each represented and strengthened their respective alliances. The bipolar international structure was in many ways, though occasionally frightening, relatively identifiable and in some extent predictable.

Following a brief period at the turn of the millennium with a single remaining offensive American superpower, humanity is again at critical juncture with seemingly complicated and unpredictable world. No one was, for example, prepared for the continuing Arab mass revolt against decades of Middle Eastern and North African dictators. In addition, the countries in Asia and South America, with increasing political, economic and demographic influences, demand more inclusive international system.

Furthermore the world continues to struggle with the phenomenon of "failed states". Such countries with collapsed or failed state institutions such as Somalia constitute a serious "threat to global stability." Georg Sørensen, a reputable profile in international affairs, believes that failed states threaten global security due their inability to provide service for citizens and effectively control territories (Sorensen, 1999). In other words weak states facilitate piracy, mass migration and extremism, in prospect not just paralyzing the concerned countries, but also potentially engulfing the rest of the world.

In reality failed states in Africa have long been fragile and lacked legitimacy. This is partially due to the fact that both the colonial and post-colonial state formations represent strange inventions for the continent. Consequently, the so-called "vampire States" led by corrupt elites oppress, exploit and victimize citizens. Moreover, the existence of a formal state apparatus alone cannot guarantee security. Currently for instance both Mexico and Syria states persecute their own people in large numbers. In comparison, when we ignore natural disasters, the number of people who die directly of armed conflict in the stateless Somalia remains minimal (although natural disasters and famine take many lives). This is mainly due to ancient informal traditional structures that ensure relative order.

In general, in a globalized world, states often lose their ability to controlling territories and people. Such conditions force states, in certain occasions, to delegate power to private companies and supranational institutions. Though the state, as an institution, lost monopoly, the dominant perception remains "State or chaos". As Collier suggests state formation takes longer and needs certain gradual construction of internal legitimacy.

> "It took European centuries to get out of a stateless condition that followed the collapse of the Roman Empire. Somalia could consolidate much faster, because unlike medieval Europe there is a modern world out there to help and a roadmap. But as long as the international community tries to run the story backwards, Somalia will likely continue to top the list of failed states "(Collier, June 2012).

Clearly, in attempts to reconstitute national institutions, Somalis seek genuine commitment from the international community in particularly recognizing and complementing existing 'successes' on the ground. The Turkish leadership demonstrated such positive gesture by initiating numerous construction projects and inaugurating commercial flights from Istanbul to Mogadishu. The Turkish Prime Minister became the first world leader to symbolically break Mogadishu's more than 20 years isolation. Turkey shares cultural and historical relations with the Horn of Africa and is therefore in a unique position to bridge the gap between the West and the Horn of Africa. Regardless of any international goodwill engagement, responsibility rests on the Somalis themselves. Somalis must democratically find out which social order and state structure that suits them best. In this regard, a more inclusive effort rather than a military intervening international order will be helpful. Such an opportunity have Somalis longed for since the Portuguese seafarer Vasco da Gama in 1500-century on his way to India attacked the Banadir coast, which was then a well-functioning cosmopolitan city-state (Subrah, 1997). This article proposes that, in order to make this time right, Somali national reconstruction efforts has to be based on civil society foundation. The formal end of the transitional period should lead to a renewed optimism and willingness to move forward.

Civil society resurrection in Somalia

In the eyes of the world, Somalia has for many years symbolized war, death and human tragedy. For the first time in several decades, the world have for the past months witnessed a different picture and a possible rebirth of a peaceful Somalia. Around the world Somalis, with celebrations and optimism, welcomed the indirect election of a parliamentary speaker and a President who later appointed a government consisting of ten ministers including to women. It was politically wise and significantly refreshing of the current leadership in Mogadishu to come up with a small government (ten ministers) including hopefully two strong women. Women had long suffered in Somalia. Although Somali women are the bread winners of most Somali households they have endured brutal warlordism and gang militia atrocities. It is unclear how the limited cabinet and promotion of women will work out in relation to the notoriously distrustful Somali clan dynamics. The daring steps by the current leadership will certainly improve Somalia's currently catastrophic international image. In addition depending on what this government does, it might help the country improving its standing on the annual global indexes so far repetitively marked by undisputed high ranking status in statelessness, corruption and abject poverty.

In this post-conflict critical juncture, leadership matters. It also helps that the parliamentary speaker, Mohamed Jawaari, is a well-respected lawyer, former top civil servant, intellectual and Somali-Scandinavian who for about 20 years have worked and lived in Norway. The President Hassan Sheikh Mohamud is a former university lecturer, peace and human rights activist. During the prolonged civil war, he chose to remain in the country facilitating the education of war torn young generations and helped the poor and victims of the warring militia factions. The Prime minister is an economist who is also a successful business man. Likewise the president appears different from previous so-called Somali presidents. He seems insightful, thoughtful and careful but nonetheless confronts pressing challenges including the efforts to balance often conflicting and competing internal and external demands. The core question remains: will the president and the government be able to command some sort of state authority or will it be locked in Villa Somalia politics. We know Somaliland and Puntland increasingly appear out of reach (acting independently from Mogadishu in almost all aspects). The South largely remains occupied either by foreign forces or extremists. Obviously the easiest way to reconstitute Somalia and thereby restore the country's dignity and future is to let the president and the government deal with challenging issues. This is a qualified leadership but for Somalia there is obviously a long way to go before - after decades of destruction – the country could stand on its own feet again. There is still widespread poverty and hopelessness, specially forcing thousands of young people to seek solace in piracy and extremism. In addition, the country is awash with arms, warlords and related gangs continuing to terrorize the population. It is therefore essential that such qualified leadership should immediately obtain full ownership of the country's political and economic control. So far, Ethiopia, Somalia's regional hegemonic neighbour, a long term ally of the United States, dominated Somalia's stalemate. It might help that both Ethiopia and Somalia have now new leadership. Ethiopia, as the largest country in the region with over 80 million inhabitants, remains indispensable and hegemonic.

Language and civic mobilization in Somalia

Colonial powers engaged Somali civil society, not just coercively, but also through discourse and language application. Both the British and the Italians utilized urban people and the educated who could speak in foreign languages. Nonetheless Somalia is one of the few countries in Africa where colonial linguistic penetration did not fully succeed. This has probably to do with Somalis' continuing resistance in not allowed total colonization and settlement of foreigners in the country.

During the military regime the use of Somali language and the mobilization of the civil society was an integrated part of the national project and government consolidation. The regime later failed to convince the public linguistically. The role of the mediating role by artists and other public intellectuals disappeared or become opposed to the regime. During the collapse the Somali language lost its application and NGOs depending on foreign funding applied more on English and Arabic languages. That has so far failed to bring the civil society and the country together.

Oratory is important in the Somali culture, also in the struggle against colonial powers and the mobilization of the civil society (Samatar, 1979). The best known cases are from the application of poetry by the freedom fighter, Sayid Mohamed Abdulla Hassan, popularly ridiculed by the British Empire as "Mad Mullah". He convinced the Somalis that the Jihad against colonial powers were both holly religious and nationalistic duty. The use of literature and oratory continued in post independent periods. Literature was important in this regard. For instance

Sayid Mohamed Abdulla Hassan used poetry and military engagement to fight colonialism.

In his book "Literature, clans and the nation state in Somalia" Ali Ahmed argues that it is through language, literature, myth and symbols we understand and construct societies. Language is thus not neutral and spoken in a vacuum. Ahmed suggests that the state is preoccupied with language, myth and symbols to consolidate its grip on power and "oblivious to subtle massages directed at undermining its power base" (Ahmed, 1996: 5). According to him language and literature was crucial in independence for struggle, during the authoritarian regime and the collapse. Colonial languages were important in the process of state formation in many African countries, particularly the framing the British concept of "self-determination" (Mazrui, 1986: 39). Later the English language played an important role in Pan-Africanism. In this regard Somali language played an important role in the pursue of Pan-Somalism.

The following author appreciates the importance of been fluent in traditional Somali rural language capabilities. Most Somali leaders commanded Somali language with rural nomadic accent. Reflecting the fact that nomads or semi-nomads dominated Somali politics.

"The PM is a well-spoken and rich in his command of the Somali language. In the tradition of Ciid and Danood accent, often heard from Idaaja, who is a repository of Somali oral history and literature, the PM clearly articulates and enunciates his words so clear that one would not get enough doses want to listen more of him" (Roble, 9th Oct.2012: Wardheernews.com).

Somalis are now fragmented and scattered around the world. Division among Somalis in regional or rural-urban differences no longer makes sense, as Somalis currently inhabit in almost every corner of the world (Bakas, 2009). We therefore need new approaches to understand civil society in intercommunity dialogue and communication. The internet technology already facilitates intense civic communication and mobilization. However such information has still to reach the younger generation born among the transnational communities undistorted. Due to improper command of the language the youth might experiment modified versions of the mother language. Alternatively and potentially consolidated Somali governments can open language schools in countries with large Somali concentrations. Here the community can go to language classes in their leisure time. This requires the establishment of global cultural offices to address and accommodate transnational communities' cultural needs. This will help the Somali leadership to address civil society challenges while empowering communities to contribute and learn more about their homeland.

Conclusion

During colonial times, command on colonial languages ensured jobs in the colonial administration. In this regard urban communities had better chances than those in the interior. The bureaucracyfunctioned with foreign languages and the education system taught and socialized young people with foreign languages. Consequently introducing alien cultures, with substantial impact on the process of nation building, divided Somalis. When colonial powers left, civil society appeared confused and inconsistent.

In early 1970s the military regime formalized the written Somali language. The regime publicly rationalized the emphasis on the mother language initiative with the nationalization and integration process in the society. The language project was an integrated part of revolutionary experiments contributing to the consolidation of power in the hands of the army. The recruitment and monopolization of cultural institutions and elites contributed to such endeavour. Later the regime lost the support by the cultural elite paving the way for the country entering a prolonged conflict.

During the civil war Somalia become an open entrepreneurship space in which the Somali language became the victim of transnational NGO expansion. As public schools disappeared following the state collapse, diverse forms of private enterprises filled the vacuum leading to the opening of madras teaching basic religion and Arabic classes, which nonetheless had no organized joint curriculum. On the other side western NGOs rushed to subsidise makeshift schools. NGO approaches, the religious and the western, under-prioritised if not ignoring the Somali language.

So far Somali political elites, both in the south and in the North, failed to enter dialogue with the fragmented civil society and communicate the Somalis with understandable Somali language. This might change as the new leadership as well as the civil society seem to show interest in engaging serious dialogue to move the country forward. The question is as Somalia and Somalis significantly transformed in the past three decades, it is not clear which language the leadership and the civil society would prefer to utilize. Obviously the application of the Somali language is the most suitable. However the scattered Somali society across the globe and with younger generations not commendable of the mother tongue might undermine such ambition. Therefore the leadership should consider the following three alternatives. The first is rather ideal in which Somalis continue to rally around the Somali language regardless of geographical dispersion and transnationalism. In this approach, part of the transnational communities will confront communicative and participation challenges. The second is to liberalize the application of languages by allowing Somalis to communicate Somali, Arabic and English making these three languages the official language of Somalis. The approach will lead to the inclusion large portions of the transnational communities, particularly those in Arab countries as well as the wider global transnational communities. Thirdly, the Somali decision makers insist the use of the Somali but provide, like the Turkey, the China and many other countries, transnational Somali language classes so Somalis abroad can learn the national language through the embassies and other official representations. This option requires substantial administrative and economic capabilities not achievable in the near future.

Finally, the success of the current leadership in Somalia and the possible reconstitution of the Somali state depends on the mobilization of the civil society through linguistic and rhetorical capabilities combined with actual pursue and deliverance of clearly stated political promises and programs.

CHAPTER FIVE

Balancing Constructive Development with Material and Human resources: Transnational community Perspectives on BRICS

Introduction

In the contemporary world, the existence of unbalanced distribution of economic, social and political privileges validates the description of an 'unfinished modernisation project' with 'instances of problematic justice' (Habermas, 1990: 108). Apart from excessive inequality, overlapping multiple transnational forms of governance prevail (Shaw, 2012). In the past, we had a bipolar world order resting on two main competing ideological frames maintained by rival states and elites. Most developing countries had the option to either pursue liberal democracy with market priorities or adjust to non-liberal systems with less space for democratisation and liberalisation. In this context, the 'the end of history' thesis predicted the 'triumphalism' of the liberal economy with relatively democratic institutions and advanced industrialisation (Fukuyama, 2014: 227). Then we have BRICS countries amalgamating into this state-centric industrialised club (Fukuyama, 2014: 227).

In contrast, the unipolar system that emerged following the end of the Cold War appeared ideologically vague but unilateral in action. The US claimed that this unipolar order strengthened the structural grip of authoritarian regimes and elites on the civic space, at least in the Middle East and Africa (Halabi, 2013: 135), subsequently inaugurating devastating new types of wars incorporating irregular privatised combatants (Khaldor, 2012). It is, however, unclear whether the current multipolar world favours state-centrism equally or generates a non-state epistemic world order for non-state actors (Shaw, 2012). Certainly the West (the US and its Western allies) confronts potential competition for global hegemony from the South (particularly some members of the BRICS) with geopolitical and demographic advantage coupled with economic momentum. The West is concerned that these states might inaugurate an 'interdependent hegemony' or 'post-colonial global economy' (Andreasson, 2011; Sidaway, 2012), in pursuing alliances and reclaiming 'lost dignity' (Fituni, 2014: 99). BRICS – and particularly China – are generally pursuing global power and possibly hegemony (Taylor, 2006). These emerging powers extract resources from and exploit vulnerable parts of the world (Sautman and Hairong, 2008; Jacobsen, 2009). They could generate benefits in the short term, but are largely unable to reduce poverty in the long-term future (Lyons and Brown, 2010). These countries could increase dependency and foster a system of 'reproduction and imitation' (Sylvanus, 2007), which would be a kind of 'orientalist approach' considering less powerful countries like those in Africa as agentless (Shen, 2009). Issues of democracy and human rights are not high on BRICS' agenda (Breslin and Taylor, 2008). The impact of BRICS in seriously restructuring a global order still dominated by Western-created political and economic structures, therefore, remains uncertain (Kornegay and Muller, 2013: 192).

On the civic mobilisation side, we have increasing 'grassroots transnationalism' between BRICS and other developing countries (Lyons et al., 2012). The developmental seriousness and constructiveness of some BRICS countries (Naidu, 2007) and their developmental aid generosity (Gregory and Fahimul, 2012) have to be considered. Popularly, BRICS countries – particularly China – are considered trustworthy and respectful role models for the developing world (Sautman and Hairong, 2014).

This chapter complements the above-mentioned research, stressing the significance and positive impact of a BRICS world order, particularly for other developing countries. Based on primary interviews with members of Transnational NGOs (TNGOs) and Transnational Communities (TC) as well comments by major newspapers, think tanks and scholars from Africa and the Middle East, this chapter discusses perspectives that are largely positive towards BRICS. Such transnational civic constituencies have traditionally mobilised and strategised within the framework of Western priorities. More recently, there has been increased civic mobility (with emphasis on trade, education and exchanges) between China and Africa, for example, as well as between India, Brazil and Africa.

Furthermore, this chapter argues that some TNGOs and TCs consider the emergence of a multipolar world in which BRICS countries exert certain influence as a positive development. For them, previous world orders failed to provide constructive development and instead fostered dependence and underdevelopment. BRICS countries therefore, particularly China, appear trustworthy role models as countries that historically confronted the kinds of developmental challenges with which many developing countries continue to struggle. In this context, BRICS brings constructive, non-normative development assistance, aiming to balance material and human resources while removing existing developmental barriers. For the critics, an economic-centric BRICS could undermine global voices and social spaces and might eventually consolidate existing neo-colonial structures.

The emerging versus the declining world orders

Public discourse remains a significant factor in generating both national and transnational social, economic and political transformations. Different arguments and approaches to the actual structural transformations in some parts of the world similarly impact development. In the world today, multiple debates and perspectives exist, some optimistic and others pessimistic. These debates often reflect the political and economic positions of the involved countries and societies. People are accustomed to the classic ideas about economic development, requiring linear evolutionary progress. The current debate on development, therefore, reflects contrasting public and policy debates on declining and rising economic situations both in the developed and developing world.

Historically, the process of defeating, conquering and colonising other countries and nations to access their resources, among other reasons, played a central role in the consolidation of the West's proclaimed superiority. At the same time, counter-processes resisting hegemony prevailed. For instance, Spain, Portugal and various countries in the Middle East were once powerful. For more or less similar reasons, the UK, US and Germany also became hegemons later. The historical temporality of a country or a nation's rise into higher or lower levels of the international/global order reflects evolutionary processes of development.

The rise of the South and the possible decline of parts of the West produced an uncertain world. The reason is that the richer parts of the world will not relinquish their privileges willingly. These uncertainties influence international economic and political developments. In practice, this unfolds in emerging disagreements among competing powers on how to respond to international events, particularly those taking place in Africa and the Middle East. The issue is not therefore whether the core declines because of the victimisation of society as a whole or what Polanyi refers to as 'to subordinate the substance of society itself to the laws of the market' (Polanyi, 1957: 71). This globalisation debate, which is often core-centric, has in recent years recognised China, India and other BRICS countries as countries emerging from 'global shadows'. This discourse, however, remains antagonistic towards poorer countries, particularly those in Africa (Fergusson, 2006: 130). Despite the core-centric tendencies, the world seems more diverse and interconnected.

Multipolar world and uncertainty

With a multipolar world come many opportunities and risks. With these new, more friendly, global powers African and Middle Eastern countries might diversify and balance their relations with external powers (Zank, 2014: 170-71). Though the Chinese developmental paradigm remains attractive to some countries, China lost credibility in at least some parts of the Arab world and Africa following China's crack-down on Muslim minorities, and China's more or less direct non-interference policy on authoritarian regimes in the Middle East and Africa (Zank, 2014: 168-69). This multipolar complexity, however, introduces different constellations of power in the world, linked to the preservation or transformation of the prevailing world economic, political and social institutions mainly headquartered in the core. The newly powerful see and interpret the world differently, and seen from a Western perspective this raises serious 'human rights concerns' (Sornarajah, 2014). The assumption is that some BRICS countries will either ignore or deliberately sideline human rights issues and civic demands, negatively affecting NGOs and the wider society.

Transformation of transnational NGOs and communities

The challenge is that centralised systems often oppress civic activities, which are vital for human progress (Ehrenberg, 1999: 201). In order to consolidate, the state needs transnational economic, social and cultural elites so that through this 'historical bloc' certain hegemonic advantages in constructing ideas and institutions will lead to a 'passive revolution' (Gramsci, 1971: 263-265). States are, therefore, aware that such social forces have the potential to 'reconfigure global order' (Cox and Sinclair, 1983). Under the West's hegemony, transnational civic advocacy and awareness created certain global social dynamics. The West often evaluated countries and nations on whether they were democratic and liberal or authoritarian depending on the level of civic mobilisation. Under such moral guardianship, transnational NGOs flourished and had influence in contributing to both national and international transformations.

The Western world has been – at least after the WWII – relatively democratic and civic-oriented, with an occasionally universalistic approach to civic engagement. TNGOs often follow the pattern of state transformation. If, for instance, states decline, NGOs' activities will also decrease – meaning that, in the era of emerging BRICS, Western TNGOs might keep a low profile. TNGOs lose funding resources when traditional donors struggle economically. Consequently, TNGOs may cooperate with emerging countries and thereby compromise some of their neo-liberal and democratic emphasis. Currently, TNGOs maintain branches in most developing countries but refrain from actively calling for democratic changes (the Egyptian case has illustrated this since the Arab Spring and the subsequent coup). Initially, TNGOs combined a core-centric institutional and political frame with a cosmopolitan advocacy approach to developing countries. The paradoxical situation of core-centric TNGOs now dealing with BRICS countries as donors has the potential to transform patterns of global dependence (Vickers, 2012). Dependence still prevails, particularly in parts of Africa and the Middle East.

Many African and Middle Eastern countries have witnessed the world order shifting from a bipolar through a unipolar and now a complex multipolar world order. During the East-West Cold War conflict, there was a bipolar world order, in which the US and Soviet Union roughly divided the world into two main opposing structures. Now again, global society (TNGOs & TC) needs to navigate between the West and BRICS. The cases of Hong Kong and Ukraine, where interest groups receive aid from the West, indicate this tendency (Wilson, 2014). In the case of Egypt, society failed to receive external support for geopolitical reasons.

African and Middle Eastern countries thus struggle to overcome the legacy of colonialism and neo-colonial authoritarian structures. External hegemony sustained both structures, originally by colonial powers and later by the two main superpowers, the US and USSR. Due to the lack of a colonial legacy, BRICS could provide an alternative featuring South-South partnership.

Perspectives on a BRICS world order

There are at least three main African and Middle Eastern perspectives in relation BRICS. The first is a relatively optimistic perspective, considering BRICS a global alliance that represents the South. This attitude probably relates to the cultural and historical connections between countries in the South. Unlike the former division between East and West, BRICS countries are geographically and culturally diverse. The Euro-Atlantic alliance that was built during the end of WWII sustained the old world order. Under a BRICS world order, developing countries would receive less conditional investment and assistance. Such conditionality constituted the norm during the pre-BRICS world order. Western TNGOs traditionally supported such conditionality, but that may change, since TNGOs seem to cooperate with emerging powers. In fact, some BRICS countries are becoming a source of funding for TNGOs. Among the BRICS there are elitist-oriented states that place less emphasis on liberal democratic platforms. It is the economic elite that dominate these systems, where emphasis often rests on industrialisation and financialisation. Under these conditions, society groups and NGOs struggle to access expressive and functional spaces, and as a consequence must accept a reduced social and developmental focus. Within BRICS, there will of course be differences between Russia and Brazil and between India and China. India is a BRICS country that, in its own way, is fully engaged in both Africa and the Middle East on multiple fronts (Suzuki, 2009). Though certain limitations and uncertainties exist, optimists argue that there is more to gain from BRICS in terms of serious concrete developmental inputs, such as much-needed investment and development aid coupled with mutual trust resting on the image of BRICS members that have been role models for other countries in the South.

The second perspective suggests that although BRICS add progressive dimensions to global development, this input will remain marginal, and there exists more rivalry and competition between the North and South over vulnerable countries. Africa and the Middle East have long suffered from similar bipolar clashes. What they now need is an opportunity to jump into developmental experiments generated by others.

The third perspective, which is more pessimistic, argues that BRICS might initially show some sort of cohesion and solidarity with countries in the Middle East and Africa, but that in the end, hegemony and rationalism based on the interest of BRICS states will prevail. This will lead to the subordination of the South, and have serious negative implications for development. In addition, BRICS countries face their own developmental challenges: their systems of development are so new that it will take time to assess their sustainability. Western liberal models have so far shown resilience, at least in liberal democracies, and they have prevented conflict and underdevelopment among advanced democracies.

In the following sections, this chapter introduces perceptions about opportunities and challenges in relation to the rise of BRICS, particularly China. Gaining constructive development opportunities is important, and BRICS provides this with generosity and less conditionality and normativity. But what about the human dimension (democracy) and the risk of market overemphasis, as well as the risk of creating negative structures?

Attaining constructive development

Developing countries have long waited for the achievement of constructive developmental assistance. It makes a difference whether donors remain normative, neutral or favourably objective. The West normatively stresses human resources (in form of democracy and civic mobilisation) as well as material resources. In contrast, some BRICS countries like China stress the material/technical dimension of development. Demography is important, as Westerners are comparably few and often depend on hiring others for international projects. Under such conditions, Western development agencies have to pay wages that could create some kind of socio-economic challenges. If one looks at this from the positive side, at least it fosters business and monetary activities among the locals. In contrast, China – as was also the case in the past – provides and builds collective institutions such as stadiums or highways, from which society as a whole benefits. As the following anecdote suggests, the Chinese bring both their own materials and manpower from China, in the process alienating certain local profit-makers.

> There was once a man who owned a restaurant in a small city. When Westerners come to help the development of that region, they use to come and deal with the locals, buy something and go. Then come the Chinese they have established their camp closer by and they never engaged in buying something, etc. (Ahmed, Oct. 2014)[2].

Despite this, China remains generous in providing development assistance. For instance, assistance from China to Africa has not only increased recently, but is also constructed differently when compared to aid coming from Western sources. In general, BRICS economic and development aid transforms Africa. One of the major developmental challenges was Africa's inability in the past to attract foreign direct investment (FDI). The rise of China and India altered this trend by increasing investment in critical sectors such as infrastructure and industrialisation in the continent (Modi, 2014: 83-84). The spread of global wealth, particularly the increase of multinational corporations in Asia, confirms this transformation (Shaw, 2014: 207). It is nonetheless uncertain whether the BRICS group significantly changes the current world order. BRICS countries remain integrated into the UN and other international institutions that they, at least for the moment, do not seriously aim to re-order (Stiftung and Haibin, 2013).

---

[2]Respondents to the inquiries of the paper originated from the Middle East and Africa and included members of two or more Transnational NGOs and Transnational Communities.

Certainly there is increased interaction and exchange between BRICS and African and Middle Eastern countries. Whether this means the start of an overall restructuring of global relations or just the diversification of dependent relations remains doubtful (Taylor, 2014: 45). There is increased NGO-isation and professionalisation (creating organisations and employees) in emerging economies. Many of these activities are still driven by donations from Western NGOs. Such donations have sometimes created tensions in the form of proxy engagements (Lang, 2013: 82-83).

Before the rise of BRICS, ordinary people's ideas and opinions were not taken seriously. In extreme cases, people were considered ignorant and poor and not able to imagine progress and even have agency by themselves. This has also changed, as ordinary people can now access knowledge and initiate relevant projects on their own. In the past, even if a country wanted to develop industry, it often took generations, but now both project-level and industrial ideas are co-developed instantly, so preliminary ideas developed locally are transformed to manufacturing realities in China. As the following remark indicates, it is not just people that adjust to industrial development; industrial development also adjusts to people's needs and priorities.

> A normal person – an individual in Africa – proposes an idea about something he needs to be manufactured. Then his/her idea is quickly transformed into a reality where the product is produced. This person found some people who will listen and take his/her ideas and wishes seriously. Such activities take place all the way from Africa to Dubai and China (Abdirahman, Nov. 2014)

The willingness to present and co-develop ideas rests on trust between societies where a legacy of direct colonialism does not mediate relationships. People don't normally consider

China, India and Brazil as oppressors and colonisers. By contrast, they see these as nations of people who historically sacrificed and managed to develop from being poor to now being among the wealthiest and strongest.

> There are new countries in the world where people have more trust. In these countries you find what you want. These countries did not colonise Africa. The other countries were colonisers. People consider them role models. People are not afraid of the people from newly powerful countries (Hassan, Nov. 2014).

From a TNGO's perspective, BRICS countries are considered role models, as the following remark indicates:

> Countries in the Middle East (Egypt) could benefit from the developmental experience of Brazil, for example, particularly in the fields of promoting justice and reducing poverty. Within a limited period of time Brazil became the 6th wealthiest in the world (Al-Ahram Centre for Strategic Studies, 28 May 2013).

Fear of these emerging nations, though minimal, is nonetheless present. Although this role model attitude prevails among developing countries in Africa and the Middle East, TNGOS caution that BRICS' over-emphasis on economic consolidation might put 'consumers before citizens', where apart from the reduction of funding to NGOs, improving democracy and human rights might fall from the agenda (Nader, 2013). Human rights TNGOs insist that profitable markets violate basic human rights, particularly when it comes to mining and land-grabbing issues (Jones, 2012). In addition, role models are a good idea, but in the end, developing countries – particularly Africa – will have to come up with their own ideas of development and not just pursue 'reproduction and imitation' (Sylvanus, 2007).

Colonialism often creates barriers for the majority of the people. In certain contexts, it was just the elite who had access to opportunities to acquire knowledge. Now, with technological progress and its spread to new emerging powers, ordinary people have the opportunity to overcome both the expense and accessibility obstacles they use to confront.

> In Mombasa, the individual gets what he wants without leaving his/her house. There is no need for long costly travels. There is established trade, commercial links, openness and exchange of knowledge. Many students study in China, for example. These students could not get a good education before (Guled, Oct. 2014).

Normally, expanded economic opportunities could lead to more openness and possible democratisation. Such economic expansion could also result in the opposite effects consequences. Some BRICS countries have tried to accommodate society in a neo-liberal, progressive environment. Such tendencies reflect society's efforts to navigate between emerging and older powers. BRICS countries largely remain state-centric and include countries not necessarily supportive towards libertarian-oriented civic mobilisation. Such countries focus mainly on economic development and modernisation, which might undermine civic platforms. The options include continuity with the status quo of the current world order and possible discontinuity and transformation generated by BRICS. It is not clear which scenario will change the world order.

There could also be ideological and conceptual continuity between the old world order and the current one. Although bringing certain change, the new world order will maintain the status quo: the continuation of the Westphalian order. The Western-dominated world order has traditionally been state-centric. It has its origins in a Westphalia world order that stresses the monopolisation of coercive power (Weber, 1946).

With the decline of the Western model of state systems, a more inclusive world in which 'shared sovereignty' and bottom-up, consensually oriented nation-building processes will emerge. It could also lead to a more uncertain world, with increased internal (within countries) and external (between countries) fragmentations. The optimal outcome could be if global orders – regardless whether such order originate in the East or the West – engage in harmonious global interactions with compromise and cooperation, a kind of prospective world order in which labour, capital and ideas unconditionally circulate globally (Brynjolfsson et al., 2014). But first, society confronts the dilemma of choosing between a development orientation with less democracy or democracy with less development (i.e., western countries will not provide development assistance unconditionally).

Non-normative development

It is this normative focus that makes Western TNGOs debate human rights and freedom of speech. Most of their normative proclamations are nonetheless limited when put to a test. For instance, during the uprising in the Arab world, TNGOs ended up supporting their own states, or at least remained passive, for fear of losing funding. The ways in which TNGOs dealt with the Egyptian military coup in 2013 illustrates this tendency. This obvious TNGO ambivalence, as the following statement indicates, frustrates the wider society.

> Western NGOs interfere a lot and they do little (waaqawdamaqashiiwaxna ha u qaban) (Mohamed, Nov. 2014).

Therefore, the struggle for justice and democracy seems to continue even under the emerging world order. The emergence of BRICS as a global power factor does not just equate a push for economic-centric development. One should also assume that some sort of democratic progress will emerge, even if it takes time. There are indications that BRICS countries will at least contribute to the improvement and democratisation of global institutions such as the Security Council (Murithi, 2012: 134-35). There is also the already existing 'grass-roots transnationalism' in which ordinary traders both from Africa and China construct economic, social and sometimes political relations (Lyons et al., 2012). Evidence also shows that, unlike in the past, emerging countries accept transnational corporations (TNCs). China, Russia, India, Brazil and South Africa now have their own vibrant transnational corporations, and are no longer enthusiastic about regulating transnational corporations and portraying them as exploitative (Chimmi, 2012: 241). The obvious difference is that some transnational Chinese companies, for example, remain state-owned. Regardless of whether they are privately or publically owned, however, such transnationals aim at profit maximisation (Chimmi, 2012: 248). One thing is, nonetheless, certain: emerging countries, particularly China, have in practice contradicted the idea that capitalist economic development flourishes only within societies emphasising liberal human rights and democracy (Falk, 2012: 277). The popular perception is that the issue of human rights does not fit some BRICS countries' developmental engagement approach (Breslin and Taylor, 2008). Nonetheless, people in Africa and the Middle East appear favourable towards Chinese investment and development assistance, particularly when China's involvement in Africa is compared to that of the West (Hanusch, 2012). While BRICS countries have emerged and ensured a substantial shift in development within their home countries and beyond, Africa and the Middle East continue to struggle. Since the end of the cold war, Africa and the Middle

East experienced a series of ruptures stemming from neo-colonial structures that under-developed the region (Murithi, 2012: 134). Some scholars even suggest that Middle Eastern Arab countries have experienced de-development. The policies of 'de-industrialisation' and 'financialisation' driven by neo-liberalism constitute the core of such de-development (Kadri, 2014).

Balancing material and human resources

Certainly development represents complex multidimensional processes involving both human agency and the accumulation of material wealth and resources. Human potential, freedom and dignity ensure development in the long term.

> China brings a lot of material goods. But they don't discuss much about human issues. The NGOs from the West they criticise if journalists are imprisoned and if rights are violated. The Chinese just work and build they don't interfere internal issues (Hassan, Nov. 2014).

Such human agency has to come from society. Civic society – and its formal organisations, NGOs – represent spaces where the ordering of society and the propagation of hegemony can be organised. For Gramsci, state coercion to impose order is not enough; the state also depends on cultural hegemony, and this can only take place within the sphere of civic human agency, where NGOs (whether national or transnational) operate (Ehrenberg, 1999: 229). Though the West has for decades provided both bilateral aid and aid through transnational NGOs channels, the economic systems that were introduced created social fragmentation and led to the marginalisation of civic movements (Obiorah, 2007: 3).

Generosity in development aid

Development aid has, therefore, not always been successful. This is related to how this aid is given and how much. Countries like China have, both in the past and in the present, given aid to many developing countries. Now China is comparatively much wealthier and one should therefore expect the country to expand development aid efforts in poorer countries. This is probably why people increasingly notice development aid coming from emerging powers such as China and Turkey, in contrast to that traditionally coming from the West. Western countries have been providing development aid for generations, but in many cases with limited success. It is difficult to predict the prospect of BRICS development aid, since the risk of such aid ending up being abused by predatory states or being pocketed by elites exists. There is nonetheless a certain seriousness in generously providing development aid to under-developed nations and funding state-building projects.

> China is generous in terms of aid and loans. They give a lot of loans and they forgive debts. Their aid is massive (Said, Nov. 2014).

Market orientation and neo-colonialism

BRICS countries have transformed themselves from being donor recipients to currently trying to consolidate themselves as donors. The roles these countries play in development have changed over the years. For instance, in the past China assisted poorer countries in infrastructure projects with an emphasis on socialist ideological platforms and comradeship with partner countries. Projects were implemented in a short period of time and in the process concerned states and societies benefitted from such support. Today China provides development aid for ideological reasons, but it is attached to investment. China pursues profitable, market-oriented economic development and in the process creates markets and opportunities for others.

> There is difference between the old China and the new China. The old China use to just build and support. The current China makes business and profit (Geelle, Oct 2014).

China, first and foremost, doesn't just invest and develop in Africa for altruistic reasons. For instance, its huge investment in the oil sectors has to do with China's huge energy needs and with its willingness to position itself in the global energy market (Taylor, 2006). China invests and contributes to development in Africa. But the discourse – mainly generated by a competing West – that China extracts and exploits the continent also has a certain validity (Sautman and Hairong, 2008). Similarly, it is argued that trade and exchanges with China only have a short-term impact. In the long term, China might create certain developmental challenges – by not seriously reducing poverty in Africa, for instance (Lyons and Brown, 2010). In addition, though we could talk about a powerful united country such as China and its global impact, we have two main groups that engage with them, in Africa and the Middle East for instance. The first are diplomats and those who work for the state, often preoccupied with diplomacy and partnership-building. The second group consists of transnational economic elites and corporations mainly interested in the extraction of resources (Jakobsen, 2009). Similar to Western perceptions of Africa and Africans, the Chinese also project their identity through the continent. The Chinese are not saying 'Africa is a scar in world conscience' like Tony Blair, but among the Chinese there exist tendencies of 'othering' in considering Africa and Africans as victims needing rescue and empowerment (Shen, 2009).

On the positive side, China and other BRICS countries formally uphold a non-interventionist approach. This contrasts with the Western legacy, particularly for a country like France that formally maintains neo-colonial structures to this day. France often intervenes in the domestic affairs of African countries. What some people might consider positive about this is that they also ensure that the states where they intervene do not fail.

> There is a difference between the West and the new countries. At least I know the French they transformed the societies and do not allow the states they control to fail (Nuurweyn, Nov. 2014).

Those enthusiastic about the consolidation of South-South relationships consider BRICS' global role vital. Since the South became affluent, expectations that this will spill over to other less affluent countries remain high. African and Middle Eastern states (as the former Egyptian presidential tour of all BRICS countries in 2013 indicates) seem interested in emulating the Latin American and Chinese models of development. The Latin American model suggests a process of democratisation in which the military and authoritarian regimes retreat from power, giving voice and space to society, while the Chinese model rests on a strong centralised state that provides public services combined with citizen control. The Chinese state-centrism could inspire the Middle East and Africa, which often suffer from weak state structures. The combination of the Latin American and the Chinese model could help the development of some African and Arab countries, since consolidating state authority is central to progress. Whether it should be a hierarchical or horizontal process remains debatable. China's approach to planning and executing programmes in short periods of time reflects its central approach to systems and administration.

China is disciplined and it is a system. They don't want anarchy. The system must work. If there is someone who will not be in the system, they have to be excluded and punished (Cali, Nov. 2014).

The fact that African and Middle Eastern countries deal with BRICS countries not collectively but through bilateral and multilateral channels complicates such partnerships. For reasons of diversification, countries consider relationships with China, India and Brazil to be relationships based on trade and technological development. At the same time, many see Russia as a potential partner for developing their armies and defensive capabilities.

Conclusion

The rise of BRICS and the increasing global power recently gained by countries like China have been both the subject of reserved pessimism and careful enthusiasm. Many consider such rapid economic transformations a short-term development and see these countries' global engagement as being exploitative in many ways, due to existing internal and external dialectics. Though BRICS countries assert a certain influence in contributing to the dynamics of global prosperity and inequality, we still have a world dominated by traditional economic and political institutions created at a time when emerging countries belonged to the periphery.

The emerging powers have relevance for states aiming to develop equally and also for global society. In particular, TNGOs and TC will have to renegotiate and realign their contradictory relationships in a world that appears to agree with pursuing liberal economic policies, and one that so far offers no consensus as to how to alter the state-society model in which to build and proceed with economic transformation. Both global society and states are, however, interested in a stable, progressive world order where both human rights and environmental rights remain protected, while ensuring economic and developmental gains.

Critics often challenge the exploitative and expansionist character of state-centric developments by China, for example. But overall, people consider the global balance of wealth and development which BRICS countries represent an opportunity that provides investment, technology and development aid as well as more respectful role models.

In the end, Africa and the Middle East need to achieve genuine ownership in development. They will have to imagine a model that reflects their own civilizations and history. Society and NGOs can play a critical role in cooperating with political systems by imagining a developmental pattern that serves most of humanity.

CHAPTER SIX

Transnational citizenship, violence, extremism and International aid

Introduction

Political violence and extremism is not just a product of warring and conflicting parties aiming to monopolize violence and power in a given country. Such terms also refer to political processes that impact on national, international and transnational connections. In what we could refer to as the politics of fear. Thomas Hobbes argues that human condition is often between "state of nature" and "state of civility" (Hobbes, 1953: 87-88). Whether it goes one way or the other depends on the social civic contract of which representatives of a given society agree upon legal citizenship frameworks. The risk of violence and extremism is always there. However for Hobbes the sovereign power is the state and not necessarily the society as such. In practice though, diverse state and non-state actors contribute to the politics of violence and citizenship. Non-state actors might determine not just the formation of nationhood and statehood but also the issue of particular communities pursuing citizenship rights. We know that non-state transnational actors engage contentious transnational political activism often applying diverse institutional, ideological, cultural and economic resources (Tarrow, 2005; Keck and Sikkink, 1998). Such resources could originate from state agencies in developing countries and also from transnational NGOs. External resources often generate competition among diverse groups that in response to such potential funding mobilize and if needed also transnationally through campaigns, protests, demonstrations, cultural events and celebrating anniversaries. It could also be intellectual and theological mobilizations. In addition, on one hand, such movements might facilitate and adjust into the demands coming from transnational actors such as the state and transnational NGOs, while on the other hand there are also transnational groups that will resist such relationships.

State and non-state actors' transnational engagements differ in a numerous ways. One obvious difference is the issue of legitimate and illegitimate use of power by the different actors. Conventionally, the use of power is reserved for the state- that should be the sole institution that monopolizes state power. This will mean the centralization of the use of legitimate power in a given society. Such jurisdictions include the power to decide who should obtain citizenship in a particular country. However, non-state transnational actors often complicate such formal state procedures.

Despite diverse national and transnational actors imposing orders, over the years, ordinary civilians resisted and persevered in difficult circumstances. Currently diverse forms of transnational mobilizations take place both from the state's side and from the transnational non-state actor's side. Such diverse efforts, however, converge in situations where the different parties seek influence and power. For instance state actors in pursuing transnational connections, often aim at the monopolization of violence and the potential creation of state structures that provide traditional forms of citizenship to the public. On their part however, non-state transnational actors aim to construct transnational forms of citizenship- occasionally appealing to common religiosity as well de-territorializes ideas and values.

The controversies of terror and extremism have dominated global discourse since 2001. On one hand powerful countries unilaterally divided the world into the "coalition of the willing" and the rest. On the other side the world confronts new forms of extremism that threaten peace and citizenship rights. "Unlike most past radical movements that were embedded in a specific society whose ruling structure was being challenged," (Falk 2003: 56-58). Consequently obtaining citizenship cannot be dissociated from the attempts of monopolizing violence. It is possible to argue that there is a link between the current transnationally instigated violence and extremism in the Horn of Africa region and the diverse forms of experimenting transnational citizenship. This chapter discusses and analyses the dialectics of this relationship. The first part deals with the complexity of transnational citizenship and how emerging transnational connections complicate the issues of citizenship and extremism. The second part explores how external actors also impact on transnational citizenship through the application of top-down developmental engagement and securitization.

Particular emphasis rests on transnational movements coping with the surge of violence and extremism in the Horn of Africa. The question is what kind of connections do such groups have with the outside world? What is the difference between transnational civic groups that are involved in preventing violence and extremism and the state centered transnational engagements? Numerous transnational movements operate from divergent multiple purposes. Thereby we cannot categorize them as unified groups. Among them are, for instance, groups advocating for justice, better health and livelihood conditions for ordinary people. Such groups also contribute to resistance movements. For instance, in the Somali case, the resistance of the Ethiopian invasion of Somalia in 2006 illustrates transnational communities aiming to protect citizenship rights in Somalia, while at the same time maintaining connections to both national and transnational movements. On one hand, this conflict in the Horn of Africa involved transnational state actors mainly western countries allied with hegemonic countries such as Ethiopia and Kenya in the region. The official objectives were to confront extremism with coercive military means, while maintaining traditional citizenship in state-society relations. On the other hand, global transnational communities mobilized in multiple locations to resist and contribute to developments in the region.

The challenge when it comes to a country like Somalia is that there exist no functioning state that could form some sort of cohesive structures for pursuing citizenship and preventing extremism. Therefore the Somali case is a special one where the contestations from diverse transnational groups could be compared and analyzed. Obviously the transnational citizenship demand by diverse communities and external state actors insisting on geostrategic political interest will continue. Transnational communities generate not just the resources people need but also the strategies to pursue better conditions. The problem is that these transnational communities obtain different citizenships and reside in multiple locations. Such groups are neither cohesive nor homogeneous but rather heterogeneous.

Transformation and Identity

The debate on violence and extremism also relates to the emergence of transnational connections and resistance movements. In the current world, diverse competing groups pursue national and transnational citizenship opportunities and platforms. In contrast states often seek to control citizens within designated boundaries. This is, however, not the case when transnational communities pursuing transnational connections and opportunities bypass or occasionally contradict state priorities. Furthermore, transnational citizenship in the context of increasing extremism and violence across the world closely link to the issue of identity formation (Sen). Powerful countries often project ideas such as the clash of civilization and the end of history in order to universalize a singular form of identity. Under such pretext both states and non-state actors commit atrocities against civilians. For instance people in countries like Iraq, Afghanistan, Libya and Somalia have long suffered due to the imposition of top down singular understanding of the concepts of statehood and citizenship. Such operations were conducted in the name of state building that will provide better citizenship and democracy. Similarly transnational extremist groups claiming to resist powerful states also commit atrocities against innocent people. Under such complexities citizens seem trapped in between state-centered violence and identity formation logic contrasted by transnational extremist violence and exclusive identity projections.

Particularly people in the so-called fragile states suffered from invasions and diverse forms of proxies. Somalia is a country in a region where powerful states had throughout decades if not centuries competed for dominance. The Horn of African nation is also a majority Muslim country. The country has also in recent decades produced substantial number of transnational communities with vibrant global transnational social, economic and political connections. In the past Somali transnational communities resisted colonialism and dictatorships and other forms of structures that oppressed people. These communities used, among other tools, their transnational citizenship opportunities to resist. On the other hand such transnational communities might occasionally sympathize with extremism. As there are no cohesive groups, many might oppose extremism and violence, but one cannot also rule out that some might publicly support extremism. That is probably why this fight is often considered as global and not something that is restricted to particular national boundaries.

Forms of citizenship

Citizenship is a formal recognition by a state or a society of an individual's membership of the concerned state or society. It also entails access to equal rights in the governance of the country. In most countries the constitution of the country states the rules of citizenship entitlement. For instance, the American constitution endows citizenship and naturalization to all persons born in the country (Saye, 1979). In the past, people also got US citizenship following annexation (Colegrove, 1921: 5).

From political and legal perspectives, citizenship includes rights and obligations for members of a sovereign country. This was not always the case, as in pre-modern Greece any person who lives in the city qualified to obtain citizenship with a right to participate in the political debate. Some cities demanded citizenship applicants to demonstrate descent relationship to the city (Dellolio, 2005: 19). This citizenship privilege did not include women and slaves. With the emergence of democratic and more inclusive systems in Europe, the concept of citizenship expanded to include earlier excluded groups such as women, ethnic and other socio-economically marginal groups. In current welfare societies, citizenship signifies the right to access the services provided by various organizations and institutions (Kremer, 2007: 26).

Bottomore (1993) differentiates formal citizenship from a substantive citizenship. The first refers to a person's membership of a nation state, while the latter implies "the possession of a body of civil, political and especially social rights". In many countries, particularly developing countries, the standard citizenship is the formal citizenship allowing people's participation in the political system and the right to obtain national documents such as passports, etc.

From restricted citizenship to expanded citizenship

The establishment of modern European states formally linked state territories with nations. Each nation had its own designated territory. For the Westphalia state model citizen is a resident person in a particular territory dedicated to a nation. Europeans who introduced the nation state model at the time strived to overcome decades of brutal religious and tribal wars. Hence, they created state and citizenship forms to prevent future religious conflicts.

However in the process of acquiring citizenship, it remains uncertain whether to prioritize, the legal, the economic or the social. It is also unclear whether citizenship entitlement should concentrate on a particular territory or beyond. In the current economically globalized context, prosperous countries in the North often express concerns on their citizenship opportunities assuming a threat from migration and *"open borders"*. Another problem relates to the emphasis on the economic dimension of citizenship. Instead of providing service for the citizens, governments encourage and create associations and communities with the aim of letting people self-govern. Consequently, new territories and relationships have emerged making people less dependent on governments and instead increasingly relating to each other. This society restructuring might appear as an attempt by authorities to indirectly rule citizens (Rose, 1996). Furthermore, contemporary democratic practices in the West focus on deliberative democracy building on three main criteria, *"inclusion, deliberation, and citizenship"*. But such citizenship roles require formalization and a creation of citizen institutions that in return will need some kind of social capital benefiting powerful constituents rather than marginalized groups (Smith & Wales, 2000).

The industrialization of the West led to global expansion and colonization. European colonial powers had to provide citizenships for non-residents and non-natives in colonial territories (Spinkard, 2005: 8). The post-Second World War order equally transformed citizenship. The most significant development came with the introduction of the so-called Marshal paradigm, which introduced the new term of *"social citizenship"* (Isin & Wood, 1999: 26). From this time onwards, citizenship was no longer restricted to politico-legal rights but also included economic and social components. The state embarked on social and economic development activities to provide and improve welfare services for citizens. Two destructive wars devastated Europe which made the need for reconstruction and rehabilitation a priority.

In recent years the Marshal paradigm of social citizenship has been in decline due to intense technological and economic transformations. The original citizenship approach idea was not just to provide welfare service for citizens. As Turner (2001) informs us, citizens were required to become *"work citizens, warrior citizens and parent citizens"*, but the world has since changed as people do not need to work to acquire citizenship as well as they do not need to be warriors to maintain citizenship. Instead, governments introduce concepts such as *"social investment"* where the state argues it will invest in citizens' education and health.

Opponents say that such future investment arguments are not about the improvement of the citizen's education and health as such. The social investment approach aims at creating the future *"citizen worker"*, making citizenship construction a process of rational economic calculation (Lister, 1967). In developed stable democratic countries, citizenship is an integral part of the political system as governmental systems directly and indirectly, creates civil society institutions that do not only deal with the state but also go beyond the state. In such constructions the market acquires a dominant role eventually leading to a democratic deficit (Swyngedouw, 2005).

Welfare citizenship came under pressure from two quarters. First, the post WWII decolonization processes which led to intense transformation including forced and voluntary migration from colonized territories to formerly colonial countries. Subsequently, many subjects from the colonies participated not just in the liberation of Europe but also in its reconstruction. Many of them decided to stay and become citizens of formerly colonial states. Consequently, migration from Asia and Africa to the West increased, additionally complicating and gradually trans-nationalizing the acquisition of citizenship.

Secondly, the processes of globalization and technological advancement made the concept of citizenship more fluid and complex (Adams and Carfagna, 2006: 127). Under globalization with intense mobility and transnational connections, it is becoming difficult to maintain traditional welfare citizenship opportunities. Recently, a number of interesting citizenship conceptualizations have emerged. In the past, citizenship was considered a direct relationship between the state and the citizen. The state provides rights and designates obligations, and citizens access these rights and comply with the obligations. With the emergence of civil society constellations, an intermediate structure emerged mediating the citizen and the state. The state loses monopoly to provide services and rights, as society plays a significant role in who gets what, when and where. The process leads to civil society proliferation, competition and even intense rivalry.

Citizenship is continuously modified and politically constructed. A case in point is the third way approach aiming to reconstruct the citizen as a morally responsible community member. It is based on the idea of a horizontal society not divided into rulers and the ruled. The problem is that the third way might favour the middle class, as citizens with limited economic and social capabilities might risk falling behind (Rose, 2000). Such processes reflect the government's attempt to construct the unity of the nation and manage the internal diversity of the society, eventually leading to the marginalization of communities (Clarke, 2005).

From colonial to post-colonial forms of citizenship

In colonial times, Africans did not have access to similar rights as those exercised by colonialists and their associates. After independence, post-colonial leaders did not change much. Many African countries replicated colonial citizenship rules, with minor symbolic modifications (Chafer, 2002: 48). They have for instance focused on government revenues frequently instigating civil disobedience especially when such resources disappear in government corruption (Roitman, 2007). After obtaining independence, some countries made minor changes moving from a citizenship based on the territorial model, inherited from colonial powers and the colonial division of Africa, to a citizenship resting on patrilineal descent (Cheater and Gaidzanwa, 1996).

African dictators have complicated the process of citizenship when they turned their countries as their personal properties. They gave citizenship to anyone complying with their political dictation and denied citizenship to those opposing them. Later authoritarian regimes paved the way for devastating ethnic and tribal civil wars leading to the de-nationalization of these countries. Currently, many of them are trying to overcome this grave ethnic tribal framing by reintroducing a national citizenship. The problem is that African people, due to resource scarcity and political disagreements emanating from colonial legacies and natural disasters, compete and unilaterally introduce sub-national and regional citizenships excluding people from a particular region to access resources and citizenship rights. This creates fractured tribal homeland spaces of regional citizenship with sub-national identities and resource competition (Kraxberger, 2005). There are, nonetheless, some African success stories. Rwanda learnt from ethnic cleansing that led to genocide in 1994 (Mamdana, 2002: 17). Through bottom up reconciliation processes, Rwandese redefined their citizenship status moving beyond the colonial and post- colonial invented citizenship categorizations based on tribal allegiances such as Hutu and Tutsi classifications. Instead, they constructed an identity resting on Rwandese national affiliation (Buckley, 2006). Another important dimension in Africa is the need to include often marginalized groups such as women, children and immigrants. Women and children are normally not included in the citizenship rights, at least not in the political and legal dimensions (Roche, 1999).

Somali citizenship

The Somali constitution links citizenship to people and not just to territory. This implies that people who comply with the country's obligations qualify to access numerous rights such as political and property ownership rights. In return, citizens will have to contribute to the country's security and prosperity by, for instance, paying taxes and, if requested, by fulfilling national service duties.

Following the independent and the subsequent union of the northern and the Southern parts of Somalia, the country's legislative body adopted laws of citizenship from 1961-1969 that reflected Italian, British and mixed model constitutions for the central government, local administrations and many legal aspects. Qualifications for a Somali citizenship included anyone who was born in the territory of Somaliland and Somalis who renounce other foreign citizenships. What is interesting with the citizenship law of 1961 is that it did not stress ethnicity as it included anyone who was born in the country before June 26 1960 to be qualified to pursue citizenship (Contini, 1969: 51).

Somali citizenship can be acquired at birth or people can apply directly to relevant authorities in the country or representations of the Somali republic abroad. Somalia had in the past granted citizenship to all ethnic Somalis living in Ethiopia and Kenya (Herbst, 2014). Similarly, due to the millions of transnational Somalis, Somali citizenship will have to be revised to accommodate Somali transnational communities.

Transnational connections and the contention of religion

Exclusive national citizenship confronts globalization and technological advancement whereby people's citizenship can no longer be limited to a particular territory or nation. This type of citizenship was possible in the past. With the emergence of transnational communities, many with homeland-oriented organizations and mobilizations, there is a need to differentiate formal citizenship from ethnic and national belonging.

Transnational communities operate at transnational level and often link to communities through complex networks both in multiple locations. In essence, they routinely engage in multiple relationships that further complicate the core issues of belonging and citizenship.

Transnational communities had in the past the option of either assimilating or suffering from citizenship exclusion leading to community victimization and marginalization. In the current world, most transnational communities do not need to assimilate due to the globalization and trans-nationalization of the world (Bauböck and Faist 2010: 300-301). Transnational communities can preserve and reinvent ties with multiple societies. On their part, states have also abandoned the idea of forcing and demanding complete loyalty from transnational communities. In the process, new types of citizenship forms such as multiculturalism, dual and trans-national citizenships emerge to better accommodate the transnational communities' multiple priorities and connections (Cohen, 1996). What makes the conditions of transnational communities more complex is the existence of two main citizenship-related paradoxes. These concern the inter-connectedness between rights and identities. It happens through the mobilization of identity and practicing citizenship through which transnational communities tries to combine mobilizing ethnicity and practising citizenship in transnational space (Soysal, 2000). For instance, such communities are interested in acquiring citizenship privileges such as passports of, let us say, a western country. But that does not mean they are interested in the basic national identity of the concerned country. Their agenda is to instrumentalize citizenship for practical reasons such as mobility and not for identity reasons. A Somali will for example insist on remaining Somali at an identity level, but at a practical level, the individual utilizes the benefits of having an American passport and citizenship. That is why communities are interested in the acquisition of external citizenship (Bauböck, 2009). Some countries strategically encourage their transnational communities to obtain foreign citizenships. So states through their transnational communities gain extraterritorial power through economic remittance as well as accessing transnational political capacity (Sheffer, 2003: 123).

Similarly, the concept of trans-national citizenship, where people access multiple citizenships, can help us better understand the transnational communities conditions. Under such conditions, communities place themselves in an intermediate position and pursue alternative forms of belonging (Faist, 2000). The link between transnationalism and citizenship involves the instrumentalization of citizenship. Through the strategic use of citizenship and migration, people plan mobility, return, optimizing financial opportunities in many countries (Waters, 2003). Because it is possible to claim citizenship without claiming identity, transnational communities disrupt the assumption that there exists a direct link between citizenship, state and nation. We therefore need to explore new forms of citizenships with multiple identification opportunities that people can negotiate (Nagel & Staeheli, 2004).

Somali transnational communities enjoy the benefits of citizenship. Actually, there is an indirect hierarchy among the Somalis where having a western citizenship is valued. Communities, through their western citizenship acquisition and dispersed family relations in multiple locations, lead a transnational life with the aim of accessing different sources and capabilities (Al-Sharmani, 2010). Somalis with no permanent residence and citizenship status suffer from the lack of labour market participation and access to social and citizenship rights

(Bloch, 2000). After committing some offences in the host country, some of them have been deported to volatile Somalia where they are confronted with exclusion and alienation (Peutz, 2006). In some European countries, people also confront religious exclusion and extremism, restricting their rights, especially women, among them the Somalis, to wear hijab and practice Islam (Bassel, 2007). Older Somalis, confront numerous challenges including language and cultural barriers making them difficult to adjust and access citizenship rights (Cook, 2010). Community organizations play a significant role in providing services for these marginalized groups. Fangen (2007) suggests that educated young Somali Norwegians who through their contribution to Somali community organization combine integration in the host country with a sense of responsibility and belonging to the homeland culture.

Finally, the issue of religion is relevant for citizenship. In Islam, citizenship concerns membership in the Ummah (the community of believers). Anyone who is a member of the Ummah should, according to Islamic principles, acquire citizenship and protection in any Islamic territory where Islam rules (Darul-Islam) (Suryadinata, 2000: 134). So in Islam, citizenship rests not on nation and national descent but on religion. The apex of Islamic civilization occurred before the introduction of Western-European state model that propagated the modern citizenship form based on nation and territory. Islam also gives citizenship rights to non-Muslims if they comply with basic citizenship requirements (Ghannushi, 1993).

Religion is particularly important for the transnational communities. Islam gives transnational communities opportunities to operate at regional and global level – by creating trans-national public space and contesting designated political citizenship (Bowen, 2004). The Muslim community's wish to acquire and pursue transnational citizenship creates tensions, mainly based on stereotypes. In this regard, transnational communities might contribute to the construction of post-national and multicultural citizenship frames (Werbner, 2000).

Citizenship formulation represents an attempt of identity construction by the state and powerful elites. National identity, Islam and ethnicity are important for transnational communities but such communities seek identity beyond the static phenomenon. There exists a generational and class difference when talking about identity and transnationalism (Hussain and Bagguley, 2001). There is a need for transnational connections research emphasising the issue citizenship. An estimated two million qualify as members of Somali transnational communities. Many of them the most resourceful with dual and multiple citizenships currently reside outside the Somali Republic.

Transnational Communities and Transnational Citizenship

Historically it remained a challenge that in Somalia citizenship is not an issue between the individual and the state. Currently there is no state as such. But there are numerous intermediate groups such as the clan and other social organizations that mediate and complicate the relationship between the diverse groups in the society. There has to be some imposed structures and funding that complicated the process- such as funding for instances coming from countries like Saudi Arabia or the US. These transnational communities with transnational citizenships will have to pursue and promote some kind of interest in accordance with the countries they attained transnational citizenships from.

Among the informal donors with substantial external direct and indirect aid include transnational communities (Boyle and

Kitchin, 2014: 17-18). Although such actors influence all states, transnational communities exert greater influence on the development of weaker and relatively stateless countries like Somalia. Though mainly contributing to positive development the negative aspects of transnational communities' involvement in development include long distance nationalism and occasional participation in spoiling extremism practices as "potential conflict generators" (Adamson, 2013).

Both at political and economic levels transnational communities influence contemporary social processes operating at global scale "in embedded social transnational networks, remittances and return, development organizations, religious networks, cultural dynamics, and political institutions" (Mohan, 2007). Contribution depends on the hierarchically ranked status of its transnational communities. There is for instance difference whether transnational communities operate from a relatively developing country like Kenya or from a wealth nation like the United States. Similarly strategic collaboration and brain circulation between different regions is important (Patterson, 2006).

In response to such potentiality, weak states facilitate transnational community resources. For instance many African states provide dual citizenship and electoral rights. The main objective is to tap transnational community resources to enhance weakened state power. It is also possible that due to state withdrawal under neo-liberalism, community associations emerge with new financial commitments in some areas (Pellerina and Mullings, 2013).

What is the link between citizenship, violence and extremism?

The main question in this regard is: how to prevent violence and extremism in a country where statehood and citizenship at least in its modern form do not exist? This is the challenge faced by for instance Somalia a country that has experienced a recurring violence and extremism for generations. Initially it was individuals and groups claiming to represent the state- whether it is a colonial or a postcolonial- that committed multiple atrocities against civilians. Similarly sponsoring, allied or rival states often supporting opposition groups also committed gross violations. Extremism also comes from the so-called transnational actors whether it is from international agencies, organized violent groups or transnational resistance movements.

Since 2001 donor countries increasingly linked international aid with security. The distribution of aid depended on potential recipient's willingness to joining the so-called "war on terror". This was a shift from the earlier strategic, developmental, human rights and poverty reduction linked international aid.

It was under such circumstances that the US and its allies designated the Horn of Africa as strategically paramount post-cold war region and in the process mixing aid with the fight against terrorism. International aid itself is not new to the region. Since colonial times Horn of Africa received external aid. Colonial powers provided aid to strengthen and consolidate their colonial subjugation of the countries in the region. The external aid empowered mainly colonial institutions and affiliated local elites. In this regard the aid undermined the national cohesion dividing for instance the society into aid dependent elites confronted by marginalized masses searching for legitimate responsive leadership and institutional development. Consequently international aid privileged the elites while excluding and subordinating the rest of the society. With countries gaining formal independence and "self-determination" international aid poured from multiple and sometimes competing sources. Such aid often targeted the newly created states consisting mainly of the elites trained during colonial times. In addition the cold war and its emphasis of geopolitical relations, provided opportunity to the elites of these countries to demand increased aid from the contradictory bipolar system. When this system collapsed in 1991 some recipient countries become either orphaned or sought renewed relationship with western countries. Among the countries in the region Somalia was the most vulnerable. As the epicentre of violence in the horn, the country had neither a functioning state nor cohesive political elite with a mandate to negotiate and secure international aid.

Historically Somalia received two types of international aid. The first was from colonial powers and cold war superpower in the form of sanctioned aid providing military and logistical aid to firstly the civilian administrations and later to the military regime. These top down centralized alliances eventually led to mass oppression, chaos and collapse. The state centric aid was supposedly based on mutual bilateral exchanges and benefits for donor countries and Somalia. The second form of aid emerged during the post-state collapse. This latest aid mainly targeted non-state actors such as warlords and militias. Neighbouring countries such as Ethiopia and Kenya with entrenched historical conflict and border disputes with Somalia facilitated and harboured warlords. The numerous experiments of holding reconciliation conferences for warlords and armed militia groups underestimated and side-lined existing vibrant civic constituencies such as non-armed groups with long advocacy record for peace and development. Evidences show that the failure of international aid has mainly to do with overemphasis on militaristic state centric security activities rather than human security and sustainable development (Young and Findley, 2012). International aid should instead aim and empower civic oriented developmental projects. This approach requires donor states as well as transnational NGOs overcoming narrow realist emphasis and the ambivalence of not fully engaging with civic elements in the Horn as well as the wider African context.

Implication from top-down transnational efforts

The consequence of state centrism and unilateral external involvement created devastation and destruction in many parts of the world. This did not provide solution to the long term problems many countries are facing. The media depicts the on-going violence and extremism as an aggression initiated by Middle Eastern and African religious militants. Responding to the threats, Western countries- particularly US projected global military, economic and political power affecting much of the world (Sterling, 2008). Following the collapse of the bipolar world system, America tried to impose a uni-polar system that presumed western hegemony and pursued a unilateral world order. Such approaches argued for the justification of U.S. primacy with the uncritical tacit acceptance by media elites (Rojecki, 2008). In response transnational social movements, with more or less legitimate grievances, challenge the status quo of the balance of power.

In addition the ambition of personal exclusive gains fuelled the conduct of this renewed violence and extremism. For instance, since the early days of the war on terror the insurance industry and other privately owned firms played an instrumental role in the management of the global war on terror (Aradau and

Rens, 2008). The unilateral declaration of superiority led to the rise of religious extremism which America in past supported to undermine the Soviets. The conflict also introduced mounting Islam-phobic sentiments in the west (Panagopoulos, 2006). Therefore the so-called war on terror reflects the failure of the presumed American dominated global order. The conflict not only immensely derailed world peace for decades but also introduced a political economy of danger in the form of global anxiety and constant surveillance. Another important aspect is that the war was offensively marketed by mutual antagonists as having a global scope. Closer inspection, however, reveals that this is not the case as the conflict concentrates on certain regions and countries with expanded focus on security and surveillance in the west. Most of the actual operations and the subsequent suffering of innocent civilians take place in developing countries, particularly in poor Muslim and African countries (Menkhaus, 2007). So the burden of the war appears not fairly distributed. In terms of human loss and displacement similar obvious difference prevail between countries belonging to the core vs. periphery, Muslims vs. non-Muslims. For instance major frontlines situate in Iraq, Afghanistan, Somalia, Mali, Libya, Syria, Nigeria, and Niger - with severe humanitarian consequences for the population of the concerned countries.

The legacy of 9/11 and the Horn of Africa

The tragic events of 9/11 paved the way for Horn of Africa's re-entrance into the forefront of the global conflict and security debates. The horrific attacks emanating from Afghanistan had major consequences for the Horn, particularly Somalia. Apart from sharing common colonial history and traditional clan structured societies, Afghanistan and Somalia share numerous similarities. Both countries represent an extreme form of failed states and with regard to development the two Muslim countries repeatedly occupy at the bottom of global development indicators. In addition the countries suffer from protracted civil wars exacerbated by hatred invested local armed factions that seem to enjoy and see no alternatives to widespread lawlessness.

In the past the Horn was, more or less voluntarily, drawn into a different but not lesser vicious global politics. During the cold war superpower rivalry, with pronounced geopolitical motivations, fostered alliances with state elites in the region. The Americans and Soviets fiercely competed for access to important strategic locations. They did this by securing formal cooperation from the Authoritarian regimes. In return the two countries donated modern weaponry and military training.

The renewed interest this time aims, at least officially, beyond accessibility to vital strategic locations. The declared objectives include pursuing terrorists seeking refuge in the region, especially in unstable Somalia. The assumption is that this country represents a legitimate governance and security threat not only to the region but to the wider international system. This shift of strategy appears to be an integral part of the wider dominant discourse of the emerging political economy of danger (Lacher, 2008). Ideally the international political system consists of more or less sovereign states or entities with some sort of internal and external legitimacy. Practically the world is hierarchically structured presenting numerous security challenges and dilemmas (Vinci, 2008).

Somalis endured a devastating civil war with massive internal and external displacement. Under such perpetual indiscriminate violence civilians fall victim to the aggression of ruthless dictatorship and undisciplined immoral militia. The prolonged dictatorship built on gross injustices and maladministration eventually collapsed in 1991- displacing large parts of

Mogadishu residents to ancestral provinces and regions. As a temporary solution, displaced politicians and elites together with local constituents created institutions resting on traditionalism. This was less than the ideal strong cosmopolitan and inclusive systems people longed for, Somalis in the autonomous regions demonstrated their ability to imagine and build indigenous social and political structures initially with lesser aid and limited interference from external actors.

America's more or less deliberate acts in Somalia include the US's support of the military dictatorship in Somalia in the 1980s and Bush senior's and Clintons' failed intervention in 1993. Following the devastating Somali civil war, some autonomous and relatively stable Somali regions emerged. Somaliland and Puntland had through bottom up civil society mechanism managed to build regional administrations, while Mogadishu and some parts in the South experienced the intensification of violence (Piles, 1993). Despite the systemic brutality by warlords in Southern Somalia, resilient Somalis filled the vacuum in creating an environment of entrepreneurship and businesses expansion. This has raised the speculation that the anarchy may after all not be bad for Somalia's development. The Eurocentric state system remained always alien to Africa and dictatorships never improved welfare but abused and reduced the common wellbeing. In Somalia the government's collapse and subsequent emergence of statelessness opened the opportunity for Somalia progressing, making many parts of the country better off with renewed vibrancy of critical sectors of the economy (Leeson, 2006). Furthermore significant changes have occurred in the nature and intensity of conflict in Somalia. Since mid-1990s conflicts became more localized and less bloody due to criminality constraining mechanism based on customary law and private security forces (Menkhaus, 2007).

This local experiment was however short lived as subsequent overemphasis on security and warlords made civil society constituents within and beyond the country subordinate. The so-called global war on terror- elevated the Horn of Africa to a superpower strategic priority. Such re-imposition of geo-political wars undermined hitherto civic engagement and achievement. Such security developments had great impact on the society as a whole. Not just dangerous weapons ending up in untrained hands with the complete absence of state monitoring mechanism I think there needs to be some considerations on the nature of the Somali state before the collapse, but also the process of unleashing widespread robbery, revenge killings, looting properties and rape became routine terrorizing communities.

In the past decades Somalis experienced death, mayhem and expulsion initiated and implemented by dictatorship and warlords. In a world where men with weapons pursuing violence attract more attention, controlling small territory and commanding a bunch of militia guaranteed certain recognition and inclusion into political processes. Consequently the so-called war on terror elevated diverse warlords and their militias into almost a partner if not an ally status. In the Somali context this was coupled with the use of Ethiopia as proxy to supervise and manage the Somali warlords. After costly experiment with huge cost, Ethiopia finally withdrew its troops. This was mainly due to expanding Somali national and transnational resistance plus change of administration in Washington that continued the so-called war on terror but in diffused form. Eventually the decisions to elevate the warlord status, the Ethiopian and US intervention failed and increased violence and extremism. Now Somalis became victims of complex net of extremists, warlords and external actors preoccupied with pursuing religious militants.

The war on terror was an unjust war. Apart from the human cost in the form of mass death and displacement. Countries invaded and destroyed hence aggravating political and economic setbacks. More seriously warlords and authoritarian rulers adopted and employed the war rhetoric for power consolidation. At the regional level animosities were created (prior to the war, migration and border businesses flourished with people in the region interacting).

Most damaging so far is the disruption of the locally created indigenous Somali order during the post state collapse. Through the combination of Xeer- Somali customary laws and Sharia to resolve and manage local disputes, many parts of the country adopted and established relative peace. Within the framework of the new terrorist paradigm, respected civil society groups in Somalia and beyond were accused of potential terrorists.

At the same time warlords received clandestine funding and became important members of the alliances of willing (Dagne, 2002). The war on terror took extremism and radicalization among the Somalis into higher levels, especially the growing concern among the youth, posing serious future challenges. The only way to prevent Somalia from becoming a fertile ground for international terrorist groups is to help stabilize the country. In order to achieve this objective, it is crucial to adopt initiatives aiming at strengthening Somalia's civil society (Tripodi, 2005).

In this regard citizens became hostages between an oppressive regime they seriously feared and obviously will not shed tears for its demise and disorganized extremely threatening armed militias. Here the process of monopolization and de-monopolization of power is important. In traditional authoritarian societies monopoly of violence rests on fear of a sovereign authority in this context symbolized by the military and the leader. When such personal authority, as (Diamond, 2008) suggests with an entranced conflict between the rule of law and the rule of person, disappears eventually the number of factions exercising power for narrow criminal gains proliferates. Therefore societal militarization impacts mostly on civilians though differences exist on military state monopolization to develop the country or military state monopolization to oppress people.

In Somalia most previous external interventions focused on the armed groups and not to improve the human security of the vulnerable population. Warlords received un-deserved international recognition with the intention of finding lasting political solution. The one sided approach on the war on terror missed to look at the efforts and the significance by other relevant non-armed components in the society – women and CSOs. Such contingents have long provided a bottom up approach to pressing social and economic issues. Inevitably in recent years, strategies seem to shift with renewed emphasis on building Somalia from the bottom by for instance providing opportunities for women and community activists. Consequently, the contribution and the inclusion by women, including those from transnational communities, had improved social, political and the overall security conditions. Somali women in the transnational communities, particularly those in the Arabian Gulf, cooperated with the national Somali Women organization before the state collapse. After the collapse transnational communities continued to provide support, though this more regionally oriented (Farah, 2012: 123).

External intervention and international aid can be positive if such activities focus on human development and human security rather than if such operations focus on military and alliance building experiments. International aid remains complex and often emanates from multiple sources. History has proven the existence of international aid paradoxes and ambivalences among states as well as transnational NGOs (Yanacopulos and Smith, 2007). African countries such as Congo and Somalia mainly failed following extensive largely imposed exploitative international aid. Consequently such aid nurtures dependency in what Mamdani refers to the "begging bowl culture" (Mamdani, 2002). In addition genuine sustainable human development requires freedom oriented approach to progress (Sen, 2011: 55-56). This includes not just fulfilling basic human needs but also the accommodation of people's abilities as active agents with intrinsic capabilities to influence and shape their future.

Although international aid replicates the current and strategic interest of donor states, in democratic countries concrete policies often depend on incumbent administrations. Moreover international aid reflects the developmental circumstances and the donors' and recipients' historical trajectory. For instance a recipient country's position can overtime improve to a donor status while a donor country risks downgrading to a recipient status. For instance China, India, Turkey and Brazil gradually moved from being donor recipients to influential donors. Meanwhile some formerly southern and Eastern European countries lost their previous donor status.

Consequently emerging economies with potentially donor capabilities might differ from traditional western donors. Not just because of their recipient track record but more significantly on their unburdened image by colonial legacy (Six, 2009). Moreover international aid often comes from multilateral sources depending not just on the donor regime and administration type but also the complex power relations in the world. Therefore international aid is not just for altruistic reasons. For instance China's current Africa engagement and investment concentrates on natural resources extraction and market potential (Sanfilippo, 2010). Potentially the rise of new aid partners such as China and India might reflect the beginning of the end of the Western-dominated world order. Pressing global challenges, however, require coordinated institutionalized multilateral solutions (Breslin, 2013).

In any case recipients can exploit international aid without necessarily fighting the presumed extremism. Due to the emphasis on security and terrorism, declaring a country's intentions to fight have often led to the uncritical incorporation of the "coalition of willing" which eventually trigger international aid to that particular country. Consequently the number of extremist combatting countries and the foreign aid these countries receive proliferated. This does not however translate to aid eventually eliminating violence and extremism (Bapat, 2011). Clearly mixing humanitarianism with securitization negatively impacts development. Using for instance USAID to empower police to fight extremism can back fire. Combatting extremism requires winning the hearts and trust of civil society organizations among them transnational communities with transnational citizenships. That is why international aid reduces violence and extremism if it targets and empowers the civil society through education and health projects (Young and Findley, 2011). Emphasis on human security makes progress against diverse forms of radicalization unlike if aid targets speculative elites and dictators. Involved multiple actors such as governments, civil society and donors should therefore jointly address socio-economic development reducing extremism in the long term. The weak Somali state attracts both extremists and dominant states as security concerns in the Horn override development. When the Horn of Africa became the centre stage of global terrorism, international aid selectively prioritized regime stability over human security. In a cyclical pattern this process fouled extremism and propagated the seemingly endless conflict and undermined citizenship opportunities in the Horn and beyond.

Conclusion

Let us assume that a country that is better managed and peaceful could provide better citizenship for its citizens, while a country that undergoes violence and extremism through recurring conflicts might not provide proper citizenship opportunities to the public. The exclusion and probably the oppression of citizens could be widespread. In this regard transnational citizenship could through transnational-communities- relieve the kind of suffering fellow citizens might be confronted with in the homeland. On the other hand some elements within the transnational communities who are not interested in peace and development in the country due to ideological or other extremist views might also cause challenges. It is obviously clear that there is a need to combine and redirect state efforts to improving citizenship opportunities while trying to minimizing threats from national and transnational extremist groups.

Such comprehensive efforts will require multiple understanding; multiple identities, recognitions and solutions. The proclaimed identity and unified nation-state centered model of citizenship generated suffering for many people. Here one needs to recognize the existence of multiple ways of governing, pursuing identity and having citizenships. It should not be uni-dimensional but multi-dimensional. There are diverse forms of citizenships and diverse forms of governance that people could pursue. There are also transnational communities with multiple connections, strategies and citizenships that need to be accommodated within the current complex and in-cohesive world.

With regard to the fight against violence and extremism, in the end the solution will have to come from concerned societies such as Somalis. External involvement will have to take place through dialogue and consent. Here emerging powers such as China could play an important role in balancing support to the state with (while) neglecting the cultural need of the increasingly trans-nationalized society.

The conflict in the Horn of Africa- particularly Somalia remains complex and intricate to resolve. In order to overcome pressing issues involved actors need to sincerely cooperate and compromise. At the moment the region needs a new approach different from the destructive and discredited past of colonialism, dictatorship, warlords and war on terror. Somalis need an opportunity and space to consider and construct their destiny. Interestingly the few occasions in the past where Somalis experienced non-interference they ended up resolving disagreements peacefully (the cases of Puntland, Somaliland illustrate this trend). Such locally initiated socio-political developments occurred without external involvement. Although Somalis produced local and regional political settlement by mixing traditional reconciliatory tools with modern civil society mobilizations, the country has still to produce national leaders with national vision for progress. Obviously Somalia is not an island and international interest and interaction will continue but a positive external involvement will rather be complementary. Furthermore it seems that Somalis might be ready to embrace a form of traditional statehood bringing religion and culture into the system. Whether the international community equally accepts such alternative models remains doubtful. Similar to many other African countries, Somalis never had, in modern times, an opportunity to establish their own independent political structures. That is probably why all imposed structures failed. The time has come to let indigenous structured systems emerge with eventual transnational inputs. A progressive semi-modern traditional platform might promote horizontal cohesion help them Somalis overcoming citizenship, violence and extremism obstacles. Paradoxically the obvious and most serious challenge to the approach of traditional governance comes from the armed radical groups in the country. They want to assert an extremist religious rule but preferably a version based on their own narrow interpretations.

Whatever legitimate or illegitimate concerns outsiders might have, statelessness, anarchy, extremism in Somalia could only be overcome if Somalis independently determine their destiny. In this endeavour the country needs its scattered human capital among the transnational communities. A new transnational communities incorporated developmental approach linked to the vibrant civil society and local administrative structures in the country would certainly constitute functioning reliable building blocks to restore stable peace and statehood in Somalia.

CHAPTER SEVEN

Transnational Community Consolidation and Mobilization: The Case of Transnational Somali Communities in the UAE

Introduction

Migration is an integrated part of human potential and survival. In classical times, scholars stressed that migration processes transform societies from *badawa* (simple rural life) to *hadara* (complex diversified urban life) (Chabane, 2008) or from stages of *mechanical solidarity* or *organic solidarity* (Durkheim, 1933: 129). Such theoretical frames assume migrants abandoning tradition and embracing the inevitability of modernity in the process of evolutionary development. Certainly, this is not the case in the current and vastly more complex and uncertain globalised environment, where human mobility follows non-linear complexities of interconnectedness in which traditionalism and modernity coexist depending on the socioeconomic and sociopolitical requirements in a given time and space. Researching such complex development should therefore aim at moving beyond static prescriptions and objective categorisation. Migration remains essential for human development and responds to modernisation that demands diversification of labour and occupational roles (Durkheim, 1933: 190). People migrate to survive and maintain a dignified life. Under such process migrants generate and sustain muscle and brain drains, gains and circulations; and it is in this manner that migration gradually transforms societies and states. Major historic transformations such as transatlantic slavery, colonisation, dictatorship and globalisation, as well as perennial civil wars, have confounded human mobility over the years (Papastergiadis, 2000: 25-26). Migration fuels civil wars and exacerbates state collapse as refugees abscond from *fitnah* (widespread intolerance and violence). Capable community members also join diverse forms of national and international rebellions (Salehyan, 2011: 171). In pursuing particularistic gains, dominant social groups and countries displace less privileged groups from their countries of origin. In certain periods, this was done with the justification of civilisation, modernisation and geopolitical resource accumulation (Mazrui, 1993: 23).

A recent sociological debate adds migrants and refugees into a precarious class in the making consisting of three main groups (Standing, 2011: 90). The members of the first are the so-called lower working class, who due to their presumably unenlightened background, risk manipulation and recruitment by political extremists. The second group consists of immigrants and refugees that often suffer from 'ontological insecurity', partially emanating from enmity by the first group but also from mainstream antagonism. The third represents a recent, emerging group of educated youth who have failed to secure meaningful employment. The diverging groups share 'the subjection to coercive workforce, constant surveillance and dependence' and often experience 'anxiety, alienation, anomie and anger'. To emerge as a unified demonstrative class therefore requires the mobilisation of 'class consciousness' (Standing, 2011: viii-ix).

In addition the concept of precarity refers to the conditions of suffering from precarious employment situations and having fewer- or sometimes- no citizenship rights. Organisationally, the term reflects the need for civic mobilisation to overcome the neo-liberal hegemonic imposition (Schierup et al., 2014).

Though having formal citizenship, sometimes, fails to secure full citizenship rights (Anderson et al, 2012: 81). For their part, in search of self-reliance immigrants try to overcome imposed labour and citizenship limitations not corresponding to their need for transnational flexibility and connections (Smith, 2010: 269-96).

Although precarity often curb access to social and political opportunities, it could also foster increased motivation and mobilisation as well as stirring creativity among the excluded (Neilson and Rossiter, 2005: 4). Therefore ascribing a permanent precarity to any group seems rather simplistic, as immigrants, through national and transnational opportunities, often seek options to preclude victimization (Skoczylas and Mrozowicki, 2012).

However the precarious assumption of affluent societies referring immigrants to the bottom of the society attains certain validity- particularly at the beginning of a life journey with restrictive social mobility. Top-down exclusion does not automatically lead to an agentless migrant given the internal group dynamics and diversity. People mobilise and create their own transnational spaces with diverse forms of capital accumulation and transferability. Countering the institutionalised 'transnationalism from above' often maintained by transnational capital flow, transnational communities often pursue 'transnationalism from below' through the creation of spaces of resistance that informally pursue grass root activism, entrepreneurship and mobilisation (Guarnizo and Smith, 1998: 5), including family and kinship spaces (Kivisto and Faist, 2010: 141).

The conclusion of this chapter- though recognizing the precarious thesis that emphasises structural disequilibrium- complements research that highlights the civic proactive dimension as well as the agency of transnational communities. The case of transnational Somali communities in the UAE attests to this fact.

After presenting methodological and conceptual considerations, subsequent sections of the chapter discusses and analyses the Somali community's migration processes, precarity and the dynamics of spaces of transnationalism responding to such precariousness conditions.

Method

A research approach often reflects the researcher's own *habitus* (Bourdieu, 1993) and worldview (Creswell, 2009: 6). Researchers combine macro structural and institutional approaches (Giri, 2006) through which one forms one's own social understanding and conceptualisation of the research subject (Foucault, 1982: 209). This entails the prioritisation of dialogue as 'pragmatic knowledge' (Bourdieu, 1990: 298). Research on transnational complexity in particular calls for the application of a simultaneity approach of closely observing transnational experiences (Levitt and Schiller, 2004).

The study of migrants in the UAE requires careful attention to complexity, simultaneity and contextuality. Though authorities formally collect data on migration and migrants, there has been no official update on the demographic composition of transnational communities (Mahdavi, 2011: 48). In employing qualitative interviews, observations and interactions with community networks, this chapter explores the development and consolidation of a transnational community. The conclusions rest on data collected between 2009-2014 during field work in the UAE, which resulted in lengthy meetings and exchanges with diverse community members and profiles.

Although the overwhelming majority of the population in the UAE is composed of migrants, knowledge on such communities and their conditions remains sporadic and limited to occasional media coverage and governmental and external advocacy reports. The lack of research is partly due to general research challenges in the Arabian Gulf, as well the difficulties of accessing the relevant communities.

Community members often need to secure *kalsooni* (trust) before participating in research activities. With a less formalised communities, the application of multiple methods is therefore necessary. This includes reaching out to traditional community leaders representing the *Huddun* (the centre that holds parts together) of the community. Such community leaders engage in a web of links with others and thereby command respect by enjoying the traditional social qualities of being *akhyaar* (knowledgeable). These communities generally prefer to engage with others via *iswareysi* 'conversing'. This implies the researcher entering into a dialogue and information exchange on equal terms.

A researcher sharing a cultural and probably national identity with the interviewees, or someone who also lives a transnational life, often provides privileged access to 'unfiltered' intrinsic knowledge. However, such insider privilege risks compromising the researcher's 'proportion of nearness and remoteness' (Simmel, 1971: 146). The insider role also confronts situational and relational complexities arising from the researcher's and the subjects' presumptions and expectations (Kusow, 2003). Nonetheless, factors such as gender, transnational community membershp, urban identity, presumed political and regional affiliation and being from a higher research institution in Scandinavia can complicate the essential national communality in these increasingly fragmented communities that have witnessed persecution and exclusion within their original homeland and beyond.

Conceptualising Migration, Precariousness and Transnationalism

In search of alternative better living conditions pastures, migrants leave their homelands. In the past, such migrants largely consisted of working men fleeing deteriorating economic and political conditions. More recently, the rise of indiscriminate violence has accelerated states' weakness and eventual collapse, thus displacing women, children and elders. Apart from the immediate impact on individuals and groups, migration therefore affects social, cultural and political transformations in both host and homeland environments. Consequently, migrant numbers increased while migration types multiplied (Castells, 2001: 118).

After resettlement in a foreign host country, most migrants and refugees confront adjustment difficulties, including economic, social, political and legal restrictions. According to Fish (2005: 86), Durkheim links rapid societal transformation to the rise of anomie, which disrupts social cohesion. For Durkheim preventing such social decline requires top down policy interventions (Goldberg, 2008). Alternatively, community generated bottom-up responses of transnationalism, whether in a homeland or a third host country, also prevents such obstacles. To overcome potential structural anomie, communities accumulate and interchangeably transfer various forms of capital, including that of social, cultural, symbolic and economic natures (Bourdieu, 1986: 252; 2000: 242).

Concurrently existing social relations, as well as dominant networks and institutions in the host and homeland environments, exert significant influence on the actual outcome of migration and resettlement processes. Members of the host society often determine whether migrants deserve accessing or losing residence permits through periodical renewals and extensions of the legal status. Therefore, the challenges confronting communities are not merely confined to externally caused anomie but also to deliberately imposed asymmetric social relations. The powerful groups maintain hegemonic social conditions through the construction of a suitable *'social order'*, often privileging the elite while excluding the vulnerable through *'governmentality'* practices (Scott and Marshall, 2009). The tools applied include systematic control of the so-called outsiders whose activities the dominant groups often consider as representing an *'additional level of meaning'* in terms of voices and agents threatening the conventional order (Foucault, 1990).

In addressing such challenges, communities employ diverse resources and strategies depending on the existing gap between community needs and opportunities in the surrounding society. If people long for cultural spaces, communities prioritise cultural and ritual activities within the community and beyond. If demands aim at political and economic spaces, the formation of socioeconomic platforms takes prominence.

Therefore, transnational communities maintain sentimental and material links to a homeland (Sheffer, 1986). Such communities go through processes of transformation, becoming *'classical, modern and incipient transnational communities'* (Sheffer, 2003: 31). This contradicts the idea of transnational communities representing *'de-territorialized transnational familial and informal contacts'* (Amersfoort 2004). This is because transnationalism refers to *'the process by which immigrants forge and sustain multi-stranded social relations that link together their societies of origin and of settlement'* (Basch Glick Schiller and Szanton Blan, 1994: 6).

At the practical level, transnationalism takes place through diverse transnational institutions, including those based on kinship and national and non-national economic or ideological affiliations (Granovetter, 1973). Transnational communities construct community spaces which not necessarily reflect 'originality' from somewhere and 'true belonging' to a particular place or identity (Anthias, 1998). In periods of crises, communities operate as movements 'seeking opportunities, mobilizing communities and framing ideas' (Sokefeld, 2006). Thus, transnational communities build on host country and homeland power relations (Umut, 2010) through cultural capital transferability, imagining and reproducing spaces of belonging in a trans-national context (Marpil, 2009).

Community members also conduct additional migration: the so-called secondary migration to a third country. Unlike the original migration, the secondary migration results from unfavourable host societies that refer immigrants to a life under perpetual socioeconomic subordination. The move is also driven by potential opportunities emerging at the secondary destination. Initially, transnational community activities target the homeland, providing remittance for relatives as well as preparing for and investing in potential homeland return. Secondary transnationalism deals with the consequences of the secondary migration. Migrants engaged in this secondary transnationalism include entrepreneurs and people involved in educational sectors, as well as jobs that demand such transnational mobility. Apart from individuals, networks and institutions, states also generate and facilitate such processes. Migrant networks as well as formal and informal institutions create and sustain these transnational social connections and dynamics. Under such conditions, the development of economic and cultural capital as well as the consolidation of legal status remains essential for migrants pursuing transnational opportunities.

Community Migration and Transnationalism

The conflict among the ruling elites in Somalia following Somalia's defeat in the Ethiopian-Somali War in 1977-78 generated economic and political deterioration and eventually led to the migration of those excluded from economic and political opportunities. The subsequent civil war and the worsening political, social and economic conditions increased this exodus. Such conflict-driven migrants longed not only for economic opportunities, but also safety from social and political oppression. Consequently, communities already settled in the Gulf and other Arab countries had to deal with the dual task of providing emergency services for their traumatised, fleeing countrymen as well as continually attending to the needs of relatives in the homeland.

People also migrated to Western Europe and North America. In comparison to others, migrants and refugees in the West acquired better legal and economic opportunities, including permanent residence status and the possibility of formal citizenship through naturalisation. Gaining employment was not a rudimentary task for most, but access to education and welfare was comparatively better. Such secondary migration also results from relatively better residential legal conditions in the West. Strategically, many migrants have invested in social, economic and educational plans by and sending children and relatives to these places in advance, intending to join them when such a move becomes a possibility.

Factors such as the continuation of the civil war in the homeland and the declining opportunities in the host country often make people consider secondary migration. Many former residents of the UAE now reside in the UK, Canada, the US and other Western countries. The rationale for this secondary migration reflects the UAE restricting permanent resident status or secure employment for migrants. Instead, the UAE imposes harsh punishment for the unemployed, meaning they risk irrevocable deportation to a homeland torn by civil war. The *kafaala* system (in which migrants must attach to a native for sponsorship) connects a residence permit to an individual's employment status.

Such a process inaugurated Somali transnational migration with transnational mobility and connections between Somalia, the Gulf and the West. This was partially generated by the continuing economic status in the Gulf. Under colonialism, the UAE consisted of tribal fiefdoms. Formal independence and political unison first emerged in the early 1970s. The British colony recruited Somalis from Aden, in the Southern part of Yemen, which was controlled by the British at that time. The first Somalis to arrive witnessed tribal clashes among emirates. Moving between tribal territories required crossing checkpoints and showing valid identity cards (Interviews in the UAE, February 2010).

The Somali migration to the UAE intensified in the 1970s due to the stronger relationship between the Somali authorities and the government of the United Emirates, which was led by the late Sheikh Sayyid at that time. Somali professionals such as doctors, nurses and engineers filled emerging public and private vacancies. The Somali communities in the UAE were relatively well organised and linked to their homeland through remittance and frequent visits (Farah, 2012: 123-24).

Somali communities share similar precarity conditions with other immigrants from developing countries in the UAE- a country with approximate 82% of the work force consisting of foreigners (Naufal and Termos, 2009). These restrictions include visa uncertainty, preventing family reunion and prohibition of intermarriage between nationals and foreigners (Hugo, 2004). For most immigrants the conditions of precarity have worsened since the beginning of the oil boom in the Gulf. For instance, within the past decade the UAE implemented governmental nationalization (tawdiin) strategies combining with extensive neoliberal economic policies making the UAE- particularly Dubai - as a leading neo-liberal global business contact zone (Kana, 2011: 146).

Somalis- though confronting comparable challenges as other transnational communities in the UAE- their case is rather special. This has mainly to do with the lack of a Somali state or government since 1991 that could have provided some sort of intermediary diplomatic role in their relations with the authorities in the UAE. An institutional vacuum that the business elite and traditional leaders had- through informal networking with the natives- tried to fill.

Furthermore the general international migration trend of families, women and children increasingly joining trans-boundary mobility diversified the demographic composition of the Somali community in UAE. In the original migration waves the community exclusively consisted of young males.

Finally the paradox with the intense neo-liberal economic activities is that though the system often favours the business elite, it can sometimes provide some sort of entrepreneurship opportunities- though in most cases exploitative- to vulnerable groups. In addition although people originally pursue secondary migration due to the top down introduction of expanded nationalization and neo-liberalization- some community members eventually return this time more empowered with western citizenship and education and take professional and business positions in the Gulf- including the UAE.

Migration to the UAE

Since ancient times, migration and people's settlements connected Africa and the Arabian Peninsula. Thus, migration and transnationalism is far from a recent development. The first decisive migration resulted from the slave trade between Africa and Arabia. Diverse forms of forced migrations and displacements across the Sahara and Sahel brought slaves exploited as labour and occasionally traded with other regions. Such an intense transnational migration pattern institutionalised the enslavement of Africans in Arabia and beyond. The Afro-Arab slave trade, though indiscriminate and belligerent, was comparatively less massive in scope than the trans-Atlantic trade (Gleissner, 2010: 228-29).

The second significant migration was mainly generated by colonialism. The British Empire transferred colonial subjects in between the territories it ruled (Lambert and Lester, 2006: 12). This followed the region acquiring an energy rich status in between the World Wars. The British recruited manpower for vacancies that Europeans and native Arabs would and could not fill. These communities, consisting mainly of Asians and Africans, maintained transnational relations with their homelands by sending remittances and undertaking periodical visits to their countries of origin. This duel transnational engagement of investing in their countries have empowered communities; as many confronted residence and citizenship restrictions, maintaining links to the homeland represented a form of insurance.

The complexity of migration to the UAE

Currently, migration to the Gulf and to the UAE seems more diverse and complex. The first group of transnationals are vulnerable migrants and refugees who braved risky travels across land and sea in search of better living conditions. Many failed to gain legality in the new country, thereby falling into extreme social and economic conditions that are usually propagated by exploitative labour conditions in the host society. The clan network represents the only insurance to which such groups could refer.

The second group is composed of the so-called transnationals who come from different places either to start businesses or occupy professional positions, not as Somali migrants and refugees, but as professionals with western citizenships. Among them include those who were born and raised in the UAE. Obviously, the UAE did not empower them but it seemed to benefit from their qualifications.

Both groups have had varying responses to the continuing transformation in the Gulf and the UAE in particular, especially as the latter aims to establish itself as a global centre for oil, trade and investment.

The UAE policy restrictions

With the decolonisation process, the UAE changed from having been a colonially ruled nation to a more or less independent country. In the Gulf, the British favoured the Somalis and Indians as employees. When the British colonialism formally ended, the new rulers subordinated migrants like the Somalis. The traditional rulers introduced national policies inviting additional labour from diverse countries even as they also implemented strict residence and citizenship laws. The regime also pursued the so-called nationalisation (*tawdiin*) of the economy and production by encouraging nationals to take public positions (Thomas, 2013: 68).

To overcome such restrictions, migrants increase transnational activities and networks connected to the original homeland, reaching to the ancestral regions within the homeland and to the wider world. The aim is to prevent potential precarity both in host and homeland environments through the diversification and transferability of resources within different spaces and networks. In an increasingly more connected world, people do not only connect and engage with the local environments, but also relate to the wider national, transnational and global frames. Obviously, people will have to take formal borders and state jurisdictions into consideration, but communities often employ economic as well as social capital to manoeuvre between bonding and bridging relationships in ensuring better living conditions for both the immigrants and their immediate relatives.

Somali Communities and Precarity in the UAE

Since the 1960s, an estimated 375.000 Somalis migrated to the Gulf (Ahmed 2000). This was initially conceptualised as *'muscle drain'*, but Somalis also entered the professional sectors in the UAE in the early1970s (Lewis, 2008: 24). Some have been in the region for generations, working with the British colony that recruited employees and soldiers from colonised territories, often pitting one native group against the other (Torton, 1974). Overtime, many individuals migrated to Western Europe or North America, or returned to the homeland (Lindley, 2010: 32).

In recent times the UAE, particularly Dubai, acquired an international trading and investment zone status (Romano, 2004: 59). Subsequently, Somalis shifted to business entrepreneurship, many investing their *xaq* (pensions) in business activities linked to the homeland. Recently, communities from the West joined as well. Such communities represent complex groups with diverse cultural backgrounds, education levels and citizenship statuses, often combining a Western citizenship status with a Somali origin.

Many youth confront legal distress as they grow up, especially those without UAE citizenship. Parents aiming to improve both the youth and the family's overall economic and cultural capital often fund their children's attending universities in the West and Asia, and more recently, in the homeland as well. After graduation, some return to attain professional positions in the UAE. Accessing western citizenship also reflects the strategy of secondary migration.

Refugee women and the newly arrived with no legal residence represent the most vulnerable in the community; with no proper housing and jobs, these groups risk exploitation. Due to the prolonged civil war groups who can be classed as vulnerable have only grown in numbers and in desperation. It was the promise of lucrative employment by international trafficking agents that lured such groups to the Gulf (Shelley, 2010: 275). Those who are fortunate might access informal services from clan (*qabiil*) members and activist women's associations.

The business elite who deal with large transnational companies occupy the top of the community. Collective homeland mobilisations and occasional festivities bring the diverging parts of the community together.

Creating Transnational Traditional Institutions

Kinship relations remain fundamental to the community's social, economic and political organisations in the UAE. Consequently, traditional leaders occupy crucial decision-making positions, giving them power in the community. The closeness and frequent links to the homeland coupled with residing in an Arab host country with rooted kinship traditions further consolidate the traditionalistic tendencies. Apart from engaging with close relatives, communities in the UAE often interact with their clans (*qabiils*) and sub-*qabiils* in the homeland, dividing the community associations into traditional and regional lines. Based on regular communications and knowledge on the socioeconomic conditions of their constituents, traditional leaders can coordinate tangible transnational community efforts, including those needed when vulnerable numbers require support.

> Among those at the bottom in the UAE, one finds young women who entered the country illegally or found their residence permit expired: They are less educated and they don't get jobs. There is some *qabiil* network that can help initially but many of them do not have support (Interviews in the UAE, February 2010).

The rationale for the persistence of kinship relations is that the system enables communities to resist actual and potential socioeconomic challenges. The informal system represents a social security net in redistributing resources from the capable community members with jobs and income to the vulnerable, the unemployed, the sick, the elders and the new arrivals. This unconventional insurance mechanism prevents social and economic deprivation. Consequently, community members perceive contribution to the community as payment of a debt to the institutional networks that helped them to overcome past deficiencies.

> People get help from *qabiils*, they also contribute. It is a kind of investment. Men lead the *qabiils*. Their decision is *xeer* [customary law]. After *wadahaldal* [discussion], people accept the verdict and pay their share (Interviews in the UAE, December 2010).

After a long, dangerous journey across Yemen and the Saudi desert, young people often arrive in the Gulf broken and penniless. Kinship relations provide accommodation, food and pocket money, helping them prevail in making the transition. Without such a kinship network, life in the UAE, a country with no public welfare for non-citizens, entails serious consequences. Instead, the traditional structure ensures dignity for the vulnerable as well as community cohesion, despite the legal exclusion and uncertainty people confront in the country. Though informally organised, the kinship support mechanism builds on Somali customary law *(xeer)* and involves intensive consultation *(Wadahadal)* and inclusion among members.

Following the collapse of the Somali state in 1991, the community in the UAE became fragmented. Before the collapse, the community interacted with the Somali state, providing a sense of common 'Somaliness'. With the state collapse, *qabiil* relationships and regionalism replaced society and state consciousness, transforming the community from state-linked to stateless transnational community.

> We were better organized in the past. We had a state and a president. When our president visited the UAE, he used to begin his visit by meeting with us and inquiring whether we had any problems. Even the UAE government used to invite us at the official level before the collapse. And our women here in UAE had a women's organization that was connected to the Somali women's organization in Somalia (Interviews in the UAE, December 2010).

In the UAE, young Somalis also rediscover their homeland in a more practical, involuntary way. Those over the age of 18, especially males with non-citizenship status, confront legal restrictions. Although they are born and raised in the UAE, many reluctantly connect to the homeland through investment and marriage. In the process, their Somali identity, including their mother tongue, strengthens. The older generation of Somali transnational communities retains the Somali language for community cohesion and homeland development. In contrast, the younger generations command the native language. This creates an intergenerational gap and tension which eventually diminishes as the youths grow older. For these young people, the connections and seasonal returns let them rediscover the significance of the homeland's culture.

Due to the fairly short distance to Somalia, the homeland's traditional leaders also visit the transnational communities, strengthening the transnational dimension and the continuity of the kinship relationship. These traditional leaders participate in host country community mobilisations. Likewise, communities invite the homeland's traditional leaders in for the purpose of structural gains in the host country and the homeland, while the leaders, due to the communities' economic power, show extensive interest in the community.

Homeland Connections

Somalis in the UAE contribute to the homeland by subsidising the education and business sectors, as well as providing remittance to relatives. The amount remitted increases in periods of natural or humanitarian catastrophe. The community's role in the homeland is not without trouble, as active members engage not only in the economic spheres but also in the social and the political spheres. This creates tensions with regard to the people in the homeland. The business elite in particular appear to profit from the vulnerability of the civilian people due to the lack of a central governing authority. The charcoal business, piracy, investing in shadowy deals such as smuggling illegal weapons and goods add to the list of insidious illegitimate businesses.

There are cases where the business elite offer accommodation, transport and luxury for members of the different Somali government. This is mostly limited to the times when they have a particular interest and objective. Business tycoons are, in general, not interested in nation and state building (Interviews in the UAE, February 2010).

Creating Transnational Entrepreneurship Spaces

The UAE has an open economy conductive to business entrepreneurship (Herb, 2009). Such conditions help transnational communities starting small businesses and pursuing international trade. Soon after arrival, most Somalis start careers with non-skilled, manual jobs, from which they save enough capital to start or join existing small businesses and trade related entrepreneurships, mostly linked to the homeland. Gradually, they replace the initial monthly remittance to relatives with activities to buy minor shares in import and export businesses or sending goods to the family in the homeland for further marketing.

> It is easy to get a job in the UAE, if one is not lazy. I came to the UAE through Kenya where I lived a while and learnt the English language that now helps me work for a cargo company. Apart from the residence permit that should be renewed every three years, there are no problems living in the UAE (Interviews in the UAE, January 2010).

In the UAE, a residence permit is conditioned by the employment (Terterov, 2006: 218). Therefore, with their ability to provide jobs and opportunities for the people, the business elite command considerable influence in the community.

Somali transnational community spaces in the UAE include the Sharjah port in downtown Sharjah. The port harbours Indian, Iranian and Somali-owned boats exporting goods to and from the Horn of Africa. Somali-owned cranes load cars and electronic materials destined for the Red Sea port cities of Boosaaso and Barbara. During high seasons, business activities around the port employ thousands of Somalis, mainly young men and women who have recently arrived. Some of them entered the country through the same port from which they now earn their income so they can support relatives back home or save for further migration or settlement opportunities in the UAE and beyond. Apart from being an employment centre for the less fortunate community members, the port functions as a corridor and lifeline for Somalia. Brokers (*dilaal*) coordinate the shipment activities with mobile phones connecting them to *hawaala* (remittance) businesses, traditional leaders, homeland-host country business elites, ordinary employees, marketing agents in China, India and Japan, and transnational community contacts across the world.

> I have thousands of mobile phones and contacts stored in my cell phone. All of them, one way or the other, link to homeland trade (Interviews in the UAE, January 2010).

The *dilaal's* connections and the transnational business deals illustrate the character of a dynamic space connected to diverse business groups within the UAE and beyond. Somali transnational community spaces in the UAE are less gendered, as the Somali women actively demand equal opportunities. Despite having fewer opportunities when compared to their male compatriots overall, women find ways to participate in the port businesses activities. They take part in the long working hours at the port while also investing in homeland-linked import and export businesses.

The transnational community spaces have regional and kinship characteristics, as the different groups in the transnational communities focus and provide services for diverse regions in the homeland. Following the collapse of the Somali state, Puntland, in the Northeast, announced a unilateral autonomy, whereas Somaliland, in the Northwest, declared secession from Somalia. Consequently, business elites often recruit employees originating from their target region. In this context, transnational communities create not just a space that reflects and links to the homeland in general, but also to a particular ancestral region in the homeland.

Apart from providing employment and entrepreneurship opportunities for the community, Somali transnational community spaces in the UAE also function as meeting and contact places for the increasingly transnationalised Somali community. The Karaama neighbourhood qualifies as a transnational contact zone. This is a vibrant enclave where many Somalis both live and run small businesses. The neighbourhood is located in Ajman, one of the minor emirates in the UAE union. In the past, native Emirates lived there, but more recently, Somalis and other immigrants have moved into the neighbourhood to access affordable housing.

In the enclave, there is a Somali cafeteria-restaurant, which is owned by a Somali man and his Yemeni wife. Like many other Somali business owners in the country, he employs Asians. His reasons for employing foreigners rather than Somalis, as other Somali business owners suggest, include the Somalis' 'instability and unpredictability of leaving work without excuse and notice', or the problems with the Somalis 'sitting in the Cafeteria along regional and kinship lines'.

Outside the Baba cafeteria, a father and a son sit together and drink tea. The young man travelled from Texas in the US to meet with his father, who had come to the UAE for health reasons and the chance to meet up with his son. They have not seen each other since the outbreak of the civil war.

I came to the UAE for a health check and for meeting with relatives. I also met my son, who is not willing to come to Somalia for security reasons (Interviews in the UAE, February 2010).

In recent years, Somalis expanded their businesses to include hotels and restaurants, providing services for an increasing tourism market from the global transnational communities and from the homeland. Such businesses came into being after cooperation between the business elite in the UAE and communities from Europe and North America. One such Somali-owned establishment is the Jubba hotel. Local Somali businessmen and Somali-British investors own the hotel that has been open for business for the past six years. The guests include Somalis, Arabs and other nationalities. Interestingly, the staff is exclusively Asian, with many Indians. This is almost the standard in the Gulf region. Employers favour Asians, mainly for their supposed efficiency and underpaid labour status in the Gulf, although it is claimed that they prefer Asians for 'discipline and work ethic'.

Transnational Communities and Mobilisation

The Somali community in the UAE indefatigably mobilises to respond to both host country and homeland challenges. In the host country, the community struggles to overcome socioeconomic and citizenship constraints. Most Somalis have residence permits with non-citizenship status, and thus much community mobilisation takes place through informal organisations. The Somalis as foreigners, individually or collectively, dare not formally and publicly criticise the authorities in the UAE. Instead, the community restricts its activities to providing relief for vulnerable members of the community.

The UAE government controls but does not provide welfare services for non-citizens. The country officially divides people into *Muwadiniin* (citizens) accessing institutional benefits and *Muwafidiin* (non-citizens) excluded from social assistance (Peck, 1986: 68). The institutional limitations inherently include the prohibition of collective, formal, political or religious mobilisations.

Despite such restrictions, communities mobilise both at national and transnational levels. They do this through mobilising structures such as gender associations, youth groups, professional networks and business elites.

Mobilising Traditional and Economic Structures

Organisationally, community mobilisation rests on the kinship network system through which the business community, professionals, associations and pan-Somali mobilisation groups interact. Particularly, the traditional leaders and business entrepreneurs play a significant role in leading the organisation and mobilisation of the community. In periods with major homeland activities, transnational communities' traditional leaders receive reinforcement from the homeland.

Such visits from the homeland attract the business community as well as women and youth groups. They show their solidarity to the visiting traditional leader and in this way, reaffirm their relationship with the homeland as well as the importance of community cohesion in the host country. Although it is an informal social activity, there exists a division of labour. Each subgroup is responsible for the mobilisation and the collection of resources from that particular group:

> If politicians and traditional leaders come here or if somebody needs help, people are *waa la abaabulaa* (mobilized) and organized properly. For instance, the business people are sent to business persons, the young

people to young persons, the women to the women (Interviews in the UAE, January 2010).

The support of the business elite is indispensable for community mobilisation. They have particularly sponsored high profile visits from the homeland and national celebration events in the host country. This is obviously a strategic action from their side, as they depend on community legitimacy and support both in the host environment and in the homeland.

The *qaaraan* (charity collection) plays a significant role in the community organisation and mobilisation. Through the collection of *qaaraan*, the community shares the potential economic burden. Each member of the *qabiil* with a job and income contributes to the *qaraan*. In return, the individual qualifies for receiving support during recession.

Transnational communities mobilise to provide charity and humanitarian support for the poor, both in the host country and in the homeland. In a country like the UAE with no universal welfare system, people depend on transnational communities for survival, so the community mobilises financial resources in order to reach such vulnerable groups. Though kinship mobilisation is dominant when it comes to community structuring, there are also non-*qabiil* based *qaraan* collections. These include networks of friends and professionals who collect and provide support for people in need.

Empowering the Community and Homeland Regional Alliances

At the subgroup level, the community mobilises its resources to reach those who confront major obstacles. These include Somali women, some of them young, who suffer due to unemployment and problems with legal residence. The community also mobilises to empower the unemployed youth to get an education. The aim is to remedy structural barriers that often lead to young men losing their legal residence at the age of 18, when they are no longer considered children. If they do not get jobs, they risk expulsion to the homeland. Individual groups and associations collect money and invite the embassy to support young people in obtaining minor skills and computer training.

Communities mobilise economic resources to help vulnerable community members such as women, the sick and youth in the homeland. In addition, they organise fundraising events for the development of their native country. This includes both humanitarian and political events aimed at supporting homeland constituents. Mobility and the proximity to Somalia make such transnational engagements more frequent. Again, a significant contribution comes from the traditional leaders and the business elite.

Over the past two decades, the community experienced intense mobilisation focusing on regional support. This is mainly to do with the lack of a centralised government in Somalia. The absence of a properly functioning Somali embassy exacerbates such community fragmentation. Prior to the civil war, the embassy played a significant role in community organisation and mobilisation. Although kinship network mobilisation provides a certain relief for many people in the host country, the system also indirectly undermines the collective, general mobilisation of the Somalis.

Capital Transferability among Transnational Communities

The legal constraints in the UAE pressure communities in the UAE to live uncertainly, with continuous planning and strategising. They undertake preventive measures, including investing in a family member to immigrate for education and for work in Europe or North America. This is not a just a project designed for the concerned individual, but a collective strategy for the whole family. The expected return is citizenship, better education, employment, remittance and family reunion.

> We are investing in the children and their education so they can take care of themselves and the family (Interviews in the UAE, January 2010).

Parents invest in their children's education, mainly to secure the future of their children but also for their own retirement. In addition, as many of these parents did not have educational opportunities themselves, they are eager to realise their dreams through their children. However, providing education for young people in a country where one has to pay for everything is very difficult. Instead, parents often invest in their children getting an education in universities in India and Malaysia, which are less expensive but still competitive.

> I grew up in the UAE and as a child went to school there. When I reached 18, my father's (family's) residence permit could not help me. I have to get my own through job or education. The option was getting higher education for which my parents could not pay or leaving the country. I was lucky to get the support of relatives to immigrate to the US. In the US, I got both education and citizenship. Now I am again in the UAE with a professional job. This would have been impossible for me to get if I did not migrate (Interviews in the UAE, July 2014).

On the surface, the legal exclusion of transnational communities appears negative, but the temporal uncertainty does cause communities to search actively for opportunities, becoming entrepreneurs and establishing businesses that not only trade and interact with the homeland but also improve the position of the communities in the host country. Communities acquire and transfer diverse capital from both the homeland and the host country to overcome the structural challenges they face. In addition, transnational communities remain the driving force of the homeland economy, as they diversify and gradually develop to a transnational contact space for the globally dispersed Somalis.

With regard to social quality of life, communities in the UAE live reasonably well. There are numerous challenges, such as the legal uncertainty and the lack of free education and welfare, but for many, life in the UAE is better than that in Somalia and many other parts in the Middle East and Africa. The kind of businesses the community conducts have changed and gradually become more sophisticated depending on the diverse forms of capital available to investors

The community recently expanded to service sectors such as hotel and restaurant branches. This move is in response to the increase of community members with cultural and legal (citizenship) resources. There has been increasing resettlement from the West and the richer parts of the world. Community members from Europe and North America pass through the UAE on their way to the Horn of Africa, and the business elite have discovered this opportunity to provide service for the global transnational communities.

Conclusion

This chapter situates community empowerment and mobilisation as a strategy to overcome social and economic exclusion at the centre of its analysis. Societies and states understandably construct legal social, economic and policy frames for controlling the procedures to include some segments of the society while excluding others. In general, such regulations impact community options. The presented empirical evidence among transnational communities, however, indicates the communities have the capability to act as resourceful agents in actively shaping their own conditions and prospects.

The case of Somali transnational communities in the UAE, often suffering from diverse forms of exclusion, shows communities creatively addressing society and state-imposed constraints. The first relates to the micro-level dynamics of linking to the homeland through relative contacts, remittances, investment and other forms of opportunities to improve social status. To achieve and maintain such a strategy, the community at the associational level constructs traditional institutions aimed at ensuring internal cohesion and solidary within the community while also providing opportunities to collectively contribute to the homeland and beyond. Second, community dynamics facilitate secondary migration as members seek better socioeconomic prospects elsewhere. The secondary migration then leads to secondary transnationalism, inaugurating complex forms of mobility aiming at moving beyond the host and homeland-centred dichotomy and providing communities with multiple choices to deal with national and territorial restrictions.

In order to better understand such transnational communities, we should work on creating alternative methodological and theoretical tools that could take us beyond the dichotomisation of traditionalism vs. moderation and host vs. home environment, in addition to examining the push and pull migration pattern.

CHAPTER EIGHT

From civilizational clash to welfare eligibility: Ethnic community perspectives on Danish coalitions

Introduction

This chapter explores the dynamics of populism in Denmark (from 2001-2011) by emphasising ethnic community perspectives and building on Habermas' (1979, 1990) and Sen's (2007) conceptualizations of publically mediated social transformation as well as Bourdieu's (1977, 1986) proposition of multiple social fields and capital accumulation. While accepting the socio-cultural conception of Danish populism, the chapter proposes a critical socio-political dimension of power and empowerment as an equally significant explanation for the process. Although cultural chauvinism provides a satisfactory account for the rise of populism and subsequent restrictions on immigration and integration policies, it overlooks the reproductive form of political rivalry within the Danish political system, as well as the choices of increasingly empowered ethnic communities. In the future, more research should focus on how ethnic communities influence the wider political process and the implications of politically active communities with transnational connections.

Diverse social policy scholarship suggests that Denmark implemented comprehensive restrictive immigrant and ethnic oriented policies involving the labour market (Brodmann and Polavieja, 2011), education (Green-Pedersen and Krogstrup, 2008), civic political participation (Togeby, 2008), liberal-democratic norms (Mouritsen and Olsen, 2013), welfare-state egalitarianism (Eggebø, 2010), and conceptualizations of identity and loyalty (Jensen, 2011). This chapter aims not to assess the content of such policies, but instead explores how members of ethnic communities in Denmark perceive and reflect the change of government in 2011 from a centre-right to a centre-left coalition. Based on the critical analysis of qualitative data of 20 in-depth interviews and three focus groups collected in 2012 and 2013, the chapter contends that due to emerging economic challenges, political overemphasis on cultural and identity distinctions evolved into welfare and economic redistribution debates. In response, ethnic communities sought identity consolidation, mobilization and transnationalism. As scholars struggle to identify a suitable framework for transnational connections (Baubock and Faist, 2010: 9-10), this chapter refers to transnationalism not as a theoretical frame but a phenomena resulting from trans-boundary social connections.

Moreover, the chapter explores the rationale of framing ethnic communities in Denmark as a threat to the Danish cultural identity as well as the recent ambiguities on welfare eligibility. The cultural threat approach represents a sociocultural populism, while welfare chauvinism posits socio-political or associational populism. Populism is a historic, multifaceted and contested phenomenon in the social sciences. It is used as a 'political rhetoric that privileges the collective action of the people against elitist threats' (Calhoun, 2002). The concept also refers to 'the establishment of the people as a political actor' (Stearns, 2008). So, in principle, populism should aim at elites rather than act against relatively marginalized ethnic communities struggling for historical and current recognition.

With the rise of populism, societies confront diverse forms of social exclusion. Distinctions of race, religion and class often constitute a prevailing master identity prone to 'overpowering other characteristics which might run counter to it' (Hughes 1971: 147). Yet, more inclusive societies eventually develop capabilities to potentially counter such obstacles by emphasising people's 'inescapably plural identities' (Sen 2007: XIII).

In responding to public discourse and anxiety on potential civilizational clash, European politicians perennially restricted immigrant and integration policies (Reeskens and Oorschor, 2012). In practice, it took place with contradicting processes of homogenization and transnationalization (Mewes and Mau, 2013). Europeans also recently witnessed outright welfare chauvinism (Aarts and Thomassen, 2008). While politicians often promote homogenization tendencies within the country, they express transnationalization needs in relation to EU and beyond. The term 'transnational' refers to activities, organizations, and movements that occur across national boundaries between peoples, governments, states and companies. The related term 'transnationalism' reflects ethnic community ties across borders, nations and states. The concept also denotes social formations projecting influence across national boundaries (Faist, 2010: 9).

In Denmark years of demarcation attempts between Danishness and foreignness prevented transnationalism opening. In response to rising populism, politicians restricted both immigration and integration policies (Hervik, 2012). For the Danes, populism reached a climax with the electoral gain of the centre-right coalition in November 2001. The coalition was the first, at least at the decision-making level, to link the civilizational cultural clash with existing welfare challenges (Hervik, 2012). Then, what started as a politically framed socio-cultural antagonism subsequently evolved into a socio-political transformation incorporating ethnic communities and the wider society. Such processes nurtured new forms of populism, nationalism and even racism. Though conceptually and empirically referring to diverse social and political activities, such ideological platforms share assumptions of civilizational enmity based on presumed cultural and religious identity. The idea of unmitigated civilizational clash as formulated by scholars sees western and Islamic encounters as 'antagonistic and irreconcilable' and ethnic communities as 'inferior, incompatible, and dangerous' (Hervik, 2004). Guided by such ideological framing, European countries such as Austria and Denmark implemented 'uncompromising' policies (Hervik, 2004).

Social theory locates such socio-cultural dialectics within the basics of human condition, where ascribed social identity confronts restrictions from acquired social identity and the inevitability for pluralism in the society (Habermas, 1979: 108; Sen, 2007: 185). This chapter acknowledges the significance of culture and welfare populism for the recurrent policies on ethnic communities. However, based on the analysis of an exploratory qualitative interviews and focus groups among ethnic communities in Aarhus and Aalborg, Denmark (2012 and 2013), the chapter suggests the power shift within the Danish society and increased empowerment among the ethnic communities as being more significant for the recent development. Apparently, there exist dialectical power politics between indefatigable political actors at the top (traditional Danish political parties) and those at the bottom (Political parties at the far left and right as well as activists among the ethnic communities).

Selected members from ethnic communities responded to the research question: *'How do you see the shift from centre-right coalition (2001-2011) to centre-left coalition (2011-) in Denmark?'* The conclusion from the analysis of the interviews suggests: a) Cultural identity and economic barriers remain the two most challenging issues for the community; b) What happened was an internal Danish political shift and struggle; c) In the process, previously marginalised parties begin to feel empowered and confident in their governing; d) Communities try to overcome such obstacles through national (creating advocacy associations and parties) and transnational mobilization (informally and formally linking to their home countries).

Research method

The chapter deals with the attempts to exclude and include ethnic communities in the Danish society. It resulted from the analysis of qualitative exploratory interviews with key informants from African, Arab and Turkish communities. Some of the interviews were carried out mostly in first languages and were translated, transcribed and fully anonymised. At the beginning, the research doesn't fully specify methods, theory or data but started with an idea reflecting the change in Denmark over the course of 10 years, going from a centre-right coalition rule to a centre-left one. Meanwhile, since 2008, there has been an economic crisis, with intense public debates focusing on economic challenges. We asked how ethnic communities understood and coped with such developments. Then, the outcome from interviews, focus group meetings and observations contributed to the structuring and consolidating of the initial idea until a consistent argument emerged.

In the public discourse, such communities, consisting of multiple interconnected personalities, often acquire diverse labels reflecting an 'implicit ideology' of blood and soil attachment (Jacoksen, 2012: 44). Apart from sharing presence in the Danish society, communities also generate both bonding and binding social capital by organizing across diverse groups, including those from the mainstream (Putnam, 2000: 23). The parochial description of communities as immigrants—though most never migrated—and the allocation of successive generational numbers—the first, the second and so on—reflects an exclusionary pattern. In capturing 'non-blood and non-soil' community dialectics, this chapter uses the ethnic community concept.

The analysis combines empirical observations and reflections, with the relevant research informing themes emerging from the empirical interviews. Focus group discussions were informally conducted with individuals who spontaneously gathered at community centres during leisure times. Listening and talking to the community allows contextualization and access to community knowledge while avoiding objectification. Although all aspects of community actions and interactions represent reasonable empirical facts (Latour, 2005; Freeman, 2004), community centres in which people discuss controversial issues qualify as spaces of 'contextualization and geographic signature' (Anderson et al., 2010: 599). However, focus does rest on community responses to the main research question. *'How do you see the shift in Denmark from centre-right (2001-2011) to centre-left coalition (2011)'*?

The exclusion/inclusion dichotomy on community labelling also exists in research. This includes community studies stressing on structural perspectives conceptualization. Others prefer active engagement and listening by avoiding pre-conceptualization and problematisation. Among the literature driven by the first approach include studies combining 'European Social Survey on general attitudes with reflections among involved scholars' (Snidermand et al., 2014: XIV, 7), those assessing secondary literature and public documents dealing with integration policies (Akkerman, 2012), those analysing political and media dynamics (Hervik, 2012) as well as the public discourse on Muslim communities (Sniderman and Hagendoorn, 2007), and those testing Huntington's civilizational clash on Danish political culture (Gundelach, 2010).

Few studies had methodologically crossed boundaries by conducting direct interviews and focus groups where data was not readily available or straightforward to collect (Schmidt, 2011; Kühle and Lindekilde, 2012). The tools of direct engagement can provide privileged access to 'unfiltered' intrinsic knowledge. Such an insider role, however, risks compromising the researcher's 'proportion of nearness and remoteness' (Simmel, 1971: 146). This chapter emerged from interviews with approximately 20 participants from three major communities with mixed social backgrounds. The rationale for the selection of the three groups was based on pre-existing knowledge of the communities and their networks. At the same time, informal focus groups took place at community centres, which are environments normally isolated from the mainstream. The interviews were recorded, transcribed and analysed for themes that were then compared and classified. Clearly, the research confronted certain limitations on recording interviews and discussions. While the inside role allows for ease in gathering and interpreting information from the community, it risks blurring the subjective voice with the analytical approach. The link between the data analysis and conclusion with the scholarship can help prevent that and provide a form of validation.

Finally, the concept of an 'ethnic community' refers to non-numerical, heterogeneous, ethnic, class, and race groups that socialize and organize distinctively and transnationally in community spaces in Aarhus and Aalborg, Denmark. Such communities share a sort of integrational conundrum as well as material and sentimental relationships with distant ancestral nations and lands (Sheffer, 2003: 3-4).

Particularization through culture and welfare

People often resist negative social exclusion while insisting on positive inclusion. The first happens through ascribed identity within the primary social group. The second refers to cultural identity procurement within complex social relations (Habermas, 1979: 108). It is from such dialectical constructs that eventual cultural hubris or harmony arises. The political instrumentalisation of cultural divergence thus leads to a civilizational clash (Huntington, 1993) that may reflect a 'clash of ignorance' (Said, 2001).

Cultural conflict emphasising ascribed identity includes the potential universalization of a dominant culture and the demonization of disapproved culture. Though alienating rival cultures reveals human instinct, it is often nurtured by instigators, not just within traditional societies but also in sophisticated post-secular and post-modern societies that rediscover culture and religion (Habermas 2003: 101-115). Democratic societies often avoid such misappropriation through inclusivity and dialogue ensuring social cohesion (Habermas, 2011: 26-27). Such societies create informal public spaces of 'cooperative fellow citizens', transforming cultural and religious demands into collective terms (Habermas, 2006).

Though people plausibly favour a preferred culture, the outcome of such choice depends on the dynamics of social interactions. As identity shapes 'our social thoughts and practice' (Sen, 2007: 35), people risk practicing 'the willful miniaturization of identity', which refers to 'the perpetual efforts of reducing people to a singular identity' (Sen, 2007: 185). Despite such a 'miniaturization' shift fostering the 'illusion of a unique and choice-less identity', one's agency with multiple identities prevails, as 'pluralistic identity is inescapable' (Sen, 2007: 86). Consequently, such identity conflicts had less to do with civilizational clashes and more with the dialectics of universalization platforms at macro levels confronted by particularization tendencies in the meso- and micro-social spheres (Habermas 2009: 228-230).

More recently, universalization and particularization debates on welfare eligibility were added into the controversies of cultural dialectics. Originally, the welfare systems of Scandinavian societies followed universalization schemes designed for the inclusion of vulnerable constituents. In stressing cultural particularization, certain political instigators have campaigned for a universalized ascribed identity to determine prospects for the inclusion into the welfare regime. Such a cultural hierarchical scheme particularizes certain members of the society—the ethnic communities, for instance—as undeserving for welfare privileges. Controversial debates of 'immigration and chauvinism of affluence' and the increase of 'xenophobic reactions' in Europe represent new forms of 'idealized supremacy' and 'ethnocentric satisfaction' (Habermas, 2009: 509-510). Challenges for democratic societies therefore include the unsettling tension that exists between universalization principles and particularization tendencies. To deal with the dialectics of 'the system world' and 'life world', societies will need inclusive, universalistic systems with particularistic sensitivity ensuring 'equal respect and solidaristic responsibility for everybody' (Habermas, 2009: 491-92).

Consequently, the combined culture and welfare clashes reflect the structural transformation of a society in which national cultural identities transform through universalization and particularization processes. The public sphere can potentially facilitate such development. Though questions remain on the neutrality of the public sphere, counter hegemonic public spheres also emerge both at the national and transnational levels (Fraser, 2014: 139-143). At least in the short term, a transparent public sphere could provide a short term solution. In the long term, however, a comprehensive inclusion of ethnic communities in the society requires re-consideration of national and transnational processes.

Ethnic communities, similar to other social groups, are not just victims of often constraining structural processes but also constructive agents that navigate in complex social fields with diverse forms of social, economic and symbolic capital enabling them to mobilize and respond to structural constraints (Bourdieu, 1986: 47). Such habitus reflects concrete experiences that shape social relations and spaces in which people, as individuals and as groups, act and interact (Bourdieu, 1977: 95; 1993). Even in contexts with emphasis on ascribed cultural identity, the agent-driven 'narrative view of actions and cultures' takes prominence (Benhabib, 2002: 4-5). Empirically, this occurs when communities utilize 'transnational social fields' ((Basch et al. 1994; Levitt and Glick Schiller 2004). Under such transnational connections, ethnic communities forge social spaces not based on pure ethnicity but on commonalities related to the contextual local environment.

In an extension of this, some community members see the disconnection of spheres, one for the mainstream society and the other for the community. As discourse operates dialogically, a process that includes 'speaker, audience and context' (Bakhtin, 1986: 121-122), such an expression illustrates community disappointment with the political system, whether it is left- or right-leaning. Instead, communities can create diverse associations that mobilize nationally and transnationally, with an occasional formation of 'multidimensional ethno-escapes' (Appadurai, 1996: 53-54).

Turning to the right

Responding to public demands, a number of European governments restricted immigration and integration policies (Reeskens and Oorschot, 2012). Exploiting public concern over cultural and welfare uncertainties, conservatives and far right political parties have valorised ascribed cultural identity, arguing for its irreplaceability for welfare privileges. Consequently, earlier marginal political parties also entered into mainstream politics.

While far right political parties increasingly gain power in Europe, minorities confront diverse forms of intolerance. Such contentions also reveal the complexity of social and economic trans-nationalization. The current welfare systems, established during a relative 'cultural homogeneity', struggle to adjust (Mewes and Mau, 2013). For instance, the recent international financial crises provoked policy controversies, including debates on welfare eligibility and cases of welfare chauvinism against ethnic communities (Aarts and Thomassen, 2008; Rydgren and Ruth, 2011). In some countries, politicians competed for the most restrictive anti-immigrant policies (Akkerman, 2012). Though the latest exclusive tendencies might reflect the economic crises, historically, Europe has witnessed excessive xenophobia both in its 'acute' and 'chronic' forms (Pickering, 1975: 328).

Similarly, in Denmark, the reception and integration of ethnic communities has generated extensive public and policy debates over the years. The politicization of ethnic communities created an alignment and de-alignment processes within the political system, with competing platforms aiming to combine 'ethnic exclusion' with 'anti-establishment populism' (Rydgren, 2004). Paradoxically, Denmark had, to a certain extent, reversed the so-called new-liberal dilemma suggesting the irreconcilability of welfare expansion with openness to an increased immigration and integration of ethnic communities (Reeskens and Oorschot, 2012). Danish politicians had, for instance, expanded—or rather, promised to expand—public welfare while maintaining restrictive migrant policies. The number of immigrants had, however, continued to rise, even as most political parties paradoxically urged the need to attract 'adaptable' immigrants that could contribute and sustain economic growth.

The Danish case also reflects a policy shift from culturally differentiating ethnic communities towards more recent emphasis on welfare eligibility and securitization (Brochmann and Hagelund, 2010: 98).

In this chapter, there are three main components. First are transnational ethnic communities that are the target of policies. The second are mainstream political parties on the right and on the left; these are not directly targeting the community but tolerating and accommodating (as Hervik's theory suggests). The third main actor is the Danish People's Party (DPP).

Successive Danish coalitions embraced more restrictive policies, particularly directed at Muslim communities. Such policy frames provided political space for the far right. Recent polls show that the party will gain 20% of the votes, enough to ensure the return to power of the centre-right coalition. Since its inception in 1995, the DPP vigorously pursued consistent anti-ethnic community policies. The party therefore inserted peripheral cultural debates on ethnic communities into the core of welfare and securitization policies. This led to increased xenophobia resting on a presumed cultural and welfare threat from ethnic communities. In response, reports from supranational and international institutions such as the EU and the UN, as well as various academic and semi-academic reports, declared the conditions of the ethnic minorities in Denmark unbefitting for democratic principles (Pentikäinen 2008: 251). The Danes also pronounced their opposition to multiculturalism (Hervik, 2012).

Since debates on inclusion and exclusion might continue indefinitely, the paradox in progressive societies, those similar to that of the Danes, is that existing democratic systems allow fluctuations to the right and to the left while constitutionally guaranteeing common consensual understanding of the core society values. For instance, the Danish turn to the right, culminating during the cartoon crisis, had the opposite result: a society willing to preserve ethnic community rights.

> ...In liberal democracies, judgements about core political rights are now anchored in consensual rules identifying which controversial groups should be categorized as dangerous and which individuals should be entitled to the benefits of the welfare state. Just so far as these rules are consensually agreed upon, they are, so to speak, part of the furniture of the political culture. However, while these rules are not always followed with perfect uniformity, they do tend to be followed by the majority of people. The outcome is that notwithstanding how most citizens feel about Muslim immigrants, decisive majorities of the populace support both their civil and social rights. (Snidermand et al., 2014: XIV).

Obviously, the Danish system and welfare opportunity structures provide spaces for both inclusive and exclusive public inclinations. Within such a paradoxical politics culture, ethnic communities increasingly mobilize, even though they might appear agentless in public.

The concern over ethnic communities

Although in decline, emphasis on sociocultural exclusion prevails under the current centre-left coalition. This represents a continuation of public concern over culture and welfare issues. Historically, the Danes described the earliest arrivals of ethnic communities, the Turks, as guest workers. In that time, the country needed manpower. However, in a time of declining economic conditions, ethnic communities became cultural, security and welfare liabilities.

The September 2011 Danish election produced a centre-left coalition consisting of three parties: the Social Democrats, Social Liberals and Socialist People's Party. The election thereby concluded a decade long, centre-right coalition consisting of two parties; the Liberal Party and the Conservative People's Party (Pedersen, 2012). The centre-right coalition had clearer strategies in emphasising the so-called value debate, mainly due to its dependence on parliamentary support from the DPP. The political thinking and planning to turn Denmark to the right was in the pipeline for some years. Thus, cultural tension in Denmark predated the tragic events of September 11th 2001 and the cartoon crisis. It started with the late Mogens Gilstrup who in 1970s initially targeted the Danish welfare system by establishing his own protest party that won a 'landslide election'. Later, he framed the concept of the 'Mohamadanization' of the Danish society, which he subsequently modified with a call for a 'Muslim free Zone' (Givens, 2005: 139). During the 1990s, with the arrival of more immigrants and refugees, such extreme orientation gradually expanded (Nielsen, 2012: 10-11). The terror attacks and subsequent interventions consolidated and internationalized anti-community sentiments (Malik, 2013: 5).

The current centre-left coalition did not fully reverse the implemented immigration and integration restrictions. It remains hesitant towards ethnic communities. With a pressure from mainly the Red Green Alliance as a parliamentary support, the coalition introduced minor legal concessions on immigration and asylum seekers, and a slight shift on cultural discourse. More significantly, for the first time in a decade, ethnic communities have (with the far left party representation in the parliament) a sort of indirect political voice. However, the changes remain insignificant, indicating the existence of wider public consensus on ethnic communities and immigration policies.

Considering these factors, genuine transformation therefore depends on the accumulation of social, political and economic capital by ethnic communities. In addition, more diversified community civic engagement coupled with transnational resource mobilization could provide the community with 'socio-cultural and economic transferability' (Christiansen, 2011).

Moving beyond cultural particularization

The complexity of ethnic communities and the competing political formulas explain the unsustainability of cultural exclusion. Ethnic communities, though sharing certain socio-political and socio-economic characteristics, represent a heterogeneous group with generational, gender, nationality and cultural differences. Much has changed since the 1980s, in which the communities consisted of insecure immigrant population and traumatized refugees. In recent years, the younger generations took proactive steps for increased mobilization and adjustment into the Danish society, but integration was far from a simple and straightforward process:

[In the 1990s] I lived and studied in Aarhus and was active in the inter-ethnic student association, whose main mission was to contribute to the debate, educate and inform young immigrants on learning opportunities......In our exchange, we would debate the cultural pressures among the Danish and ethnic minorities, but also the right to be a part of the Danish society as immigrants (In those days people called us the second-generation of immigrants (Yildis Akdogan, Berlingske, 22-01-2014).

The mobilized sections of the community include those with a political ambition. Utilizing opportunity structures, such as educational, welfare and democratic platforms combined with transnational networking, such political aspirants seem willing to compete with others even with a controversial issue such as nationalism. Obviously, the type of nationalism aimed at by ethnic community politicians represents the opposite of the one proclaimed by the far right. A good example of this development is a new political party established by communities connected to ancestral land while considering Denmark as a permanent home. In 2005, during the devastating earthquake in Pakistan, such communities organized a nationwide fundraising aid concert for the victims. Emphasising the need for a creative political platform, the leader of the new National Party suggests the following:

> We have created the National Party, a nationwide party whose vision is to promote a society where the true Danish values of respect, tolerance and peaceful coexistence are in focus. This is the vision of a diverse society where all in reality have equal rights and opportunities as citizens. We believe in the constitution and want an inclusive society where everyone, regardless of background or social status, should feel that they have a place in society (President of the National Party - Kashif Ahmad Oct. 2014*).*

The proclamation together with the objectives and the logo of the new party, which is a Danish flag, crystalizes the entrenched contest on the definition of Danishness. These are the so-called second, probably third, generation community members insisting on having a vision for a country they consider as their own while simultaneously maintaining a relationship with their ancestral countries. Obviously, the new party and the sponsoring transnational actors represent the clearest challenge to static, ascribed identity, thereby confirming the proposition of Stuart Hall:

> ...Cultural identity...is a matter of "becoming" as well as "being." It belongs to the future as much as to the past. It is not something which already exists, transcending place, time, history and culture. ...Far from being eternally fixed in some essentialized past, [cultural identities] are subject to the continuous "play" of history, culture, and power (Hall: 1990:225).

The aim of such a political move is also to remedy decades-long social injustices, as indicated by the following response from Kashif Ahmed when a journalist asked the leader of the new party to explain the rationale for its establishment:

> We have a discourse in the society where immigrants and their descendants are increasingly being made negative objects. The rhetoric has become so extreme that we needed to do something to defend the Danish values that our own parents met when they came to Denmark, a country we consider as our fatherland (Kashif Ahmed to Politiken, 15. Oct. 2014).

The process of social antagonism, which the new party decries, has been an integrated part of the wider power dynamics in the society. The Danish liberals have out of power since the 1920s, periods in which the Social Democrats dominated politics. To change this, the liberals have, in recent years, projected themselves as guardians of the welfare state in the process of entering alliances with the far-right. On their part, the Social democrats gradually internalized propositions that combine the survival of the Danish welfare state with restrictive immigration and integration policies. With the intensification of the 'value debate' during the 1990s, the welfare-integration policy link became part of the centre-right coalition's 'winning formula' under which the so-called clash of civilization attained mainstream status.

The socio-economic position of ethnic communities, particularly the Muslim community, also contributes to their victimization by the prevailing political actors in the power struggle. Many live in social housing, confront pervasive underemployment or take unskilled jobs. For the political elite, dealing harshly towards ethnic communities constitutes part of the process of gaining or losing power, in 'a site of elite power demonstration' (Foucault, 1980). In such a context, the Danish centre-right coalition gained power in 2001 due to its harshness towards the communities. The centre-left coalition accessed power in 2011 following its strategic ability to restrain the so-called Muslim 'problem' becoming a top election issue, partially aiming to bring the Socialist People's Party and the Red-Green Party on board. The long term outcome of the so-called civilizational clash is therefore the transformation of the society, not just with regard to the division of intellectuals and cultural elites into proponents and opponents of cosmopolitanism, but also in the form of minor 'protest' political parties exercising greater legislative power (Sommer et al. 2009). Over the years, populists profiled ethnic communities as a threat to Danishness and to the Danish welfare system. Even the native Danes, who reject such populism, were ridiculed as 'cultural radicals'. Thus, the clash evolved into 'a long-lasting estrangement and division within the Danish society into forces respectively sympathetic and those remaining sceptical to modernity' (Laursen 2007: 265-274).

Far right groups consider ethnic communities representing a 'parallel society'. On their part, though distinct, communities often seek commonality with the surrounding society while allowing enough flexibility to maintain their cultural difference. Achieving an inclusive transformational structure will therefore require the facilitation of people's dreams:

> People talk about integration but they also talk about assimilation. People can integrate but also keep their culture. We should give people opportunities to mix cultures. People think that people have no dreams (Interviews in Aarhus, 20 March 2012).

The economic crises as the collective enemy

The Danish centre-right coalition utilized culture, securitization and welfare schemes to consolidate its power. During this process, universalization and particularization attempts dominated political strategies. The 2011 Danish general election ended the reign of centre-right coalition and inaugurated a centre-left coalition led by Social Democratic Party and Social Liberals. However, in policy terms, the change of guards at the top was far from transformational:

> The current government has solved some minor legal issues. Now, people are getting out of asylum camps, they are getting a residence permit and it has become easier to get citizenship etc. There were problems with all the legal aspects, previously. So they did something with regard to (introduktionsydelser) [the amount of money given to new arrivals]. Culturally, they not attacking and they are not defending. (Interviews in Aarhus, 23 September 2012).

Ethnic communities expected a change on both the cultural, legal and economic aspects. Despite the adjustment of certain 'symbolic policies' on immigration and integration issues, negative cultural discourse prevailed:

Minsters still use the rhetoric of us and them. There were cases when there are taxation problems with some immigrants, the [former] minister Karen Haagerup said that people should open their suitcases and they need to integrate. So some sort of rhetoric continues. The problem is still the same. (Interviews in Aarhus, 23 September 2012).

In other words, when it comes to cultural emphasis and the demonization of certain members of the communities, there seems continuity rather than discontinuity, both from the government side as well as from the opposition. For instance, among the leaders of the centre-right coalition, political and social categorization continues to follow through ethnic, cultural and religious lines:

The people that we know can easily adapt in Denmark… for example, an American Christian, should have easier access to come here than, for example, he who comes from Somalia.
(Inger Støjberg, Spokesperson for Danish Liberal Party and former employment Minister (in an interview with Danish Public TV- TV Avisen, Monday 28th July 2014)

Although the new, supposedly progressive coalition took power, cultural antagonism towards ethnic communities persists. In the past, such cultural antagonism (or clash of civilization) rested on "intrinsic triviality", the so-called "cultural worriers" from all sides exploiting this tendentious vulnerability (Sen, 2007). The cultural antagonism reflected asymmetric power relations and structure in the society:

What happened was not an equal civilizational clash or debate. It was not a civilizational debate but a civilizational conflict. People should debate equally; it was not equal. (Interviews in Aarhus, 12 October 2012).

Under such unbalanced civilizational discourse often dominated by macro political actors, communities had limited opportunities to frame ideas. It took a dramatic transnational event like the cartoon crisis to turn the situation around. The crises and the wider transnational attention it received made both policy makers and ordinary citizens aware of the transnational and global consequences of nationally framed cultural antagonism (lindekilde, 2010).

> The problem still exists. The mentality of the Danish has also shifted; before they used to talk about terrorism and conflict, and now they talk about dialogue. Denmark became the centre of the Anti-Islamic movement, but the process had enlightened the Danish. The issue is not Islam now, but how to enter a dialogue. (Interviews in Aarhus, 12 October 2012).

So far, the political choice falls between a culturally offensive but employment accommodating centre-right coalition, and a centre-left coalition that is culturally less offensive but has declining employment opportunities. Though the economic crisis provides a break from the cultural obsession, taking the society beyond the particularization trap requires greater efforts and concession from involved parties.

> In the legal dimension, some changes are taking place; culturally, they not attacking and they are not defending. (Interviews in Aarhus, 25 September 2012).

Among the ethnic communities, the most to suffer from the economic focus and austerity measures are those with less social and economic capital, or those who depend on the welfare system in preserving a sort of dignified life:

> The current government has worsened the condition of immigrants. People began to lose their welfare benefits, especially families. In general, getting jobs became difficult and exclusion of minorities intensified. The government is doing badly in many areas. There is not more tolerance, but now people focus on something else. This is linked to the economic crises. It is important to have an enemy on the hands; now, the economy

is the enemy. The immigrant debate will not disappear because immigrants will not disappear (Interviews in Aarhus, 20 March 2012).

The pursuit of political power

Both centre-right and centre-left coalitions instrumentally exploited cultural differences and the welfare eligibility debate. The amplified emphasis on socio-cultural particularization and subsequent restrictive policies contradict the complex community identities. The younger generations often disturbs such particularization images. With their diverse cultural capital, these young people pursue creativity and diversification within their community and beyond. While the early immigrants in Denmark often occupied non-skilled positions, increasing numbers of the younger generation pursue entrepreneurship and higher education, ensuring better economic, social and cultural status (Rytter, 2011). Therefore, a change will have to come from the more empowered in the community.

At the policy level, with a centre-left coalition, ethnic minorities felt relieved from the decade long negative anti-immigrant discourse. The community, similar to the rest of the society, following the economic crises, worried over job opportunities as well as the centre-left coalition's ideological inconsistence. Even though the previous government, which was led by the centre-right coalition, pursued restrictive immigration policies, especially targeting recent arrivals, people had had better employment and educational opportunities under it. This was due to the combination of the so-called carrots and sticks (Andersen, 2011). With a centre-left coalition, unemployment among ethnic communities rose from 9% to 16%. Among the native Danes, it rose from about 2% to about 5%, where it is now. Often, ethnic minorities suffer from the so-called 'Cuckoo effect' wherein economic crises cause Danes to return to the unskilled labour positions that many typically abandon during periods of economic boom (Andersen, 2012-information 18-08-2012).

At the discourse level, the intense internal Danish debate, known as 'the value debate', partially ended following the defeat of the centre-right coalition in 2011. Since then, conservative constituents have called for the revitalization of the 'value debate'. This was a vaguely formulated discourse bringing people from the left, including intellectuals, writers, media people and artists, into ideological confrontation with members from the social conservative right. The struggle was therefore waged over electoral votes and power in an uncertain society (Nielsen 2012: 1).

> There is all this naiveté when it comes who the Muslims are? People think 'when you are a Muslim, you are an extremist' without understanding what the Islamic values are. Islam by itself means peace, but people do not get these interpretation and they get what extremists are saying. They don't understand what governs Islam. The attitudes come out of naiveté (Interviews in Aarhus, 20 October 2012).

The change of the political power at the top led to a slight shift from the sociocultural emphasis. Such developments include the electoral political system bringing practical legislative changes. The new centre-left coalition managed to make minor policy changes with less cultural rhetoric.

> The previous government had clearer policies, while the current has, so far, no clear-cut policies towards immigrants. The last government was government. There were plenty of jobs (Interviews in Aarhus 23 September 2012).

The move satisfied neither the wider society in terms of pre-election promises, nor ethnic communities in terms of revoking implemented anti-immigrant policies.

> In the previous government, it was the [DPP] that manipulated the policies. They were the ones that were pushing for anti-Islamic and anti-immigrant attitudes. Now they are in opposition. They still push for those things, but they are out of power. Instead, immigrants and Muslims have political parties that speak on their behalf. Before, no one in the government took care of their interest (Interviews in Aarhus, 23 September 2012).

Empowerment of ethnic communities, far left and far right parties

Given that politically competing constituents have considered ethnic communities as objects, it is clear that multiple complementary and contradictory spheres exist in the society. The first is the ethnic community sphere in which diverse community networks create hyphenated social, religious and cultural platforms. This reflects an acquired identity based on both socio-cultural and socio-political mobilization facilitated by the opportunity structures in the society. Included in this sphere is also the transnational frame under which the community and their diverse networks cooperate across borders. The transnational frame seeks to balance the universalization tendencies and the diversification platforms.

The Danish mainstream sphere from which the far right and far left political parties declare their wish to govern the country represents a significant structural change. Historically, this assures a serious political transformation and power shift in the society.

> The changes in Denmark is that components in the society that never thought that they would join the government are now preparing themselves for government; in the past, it was the conservatives and the social democrats that use to govern (Interviews in Aarhus, 15 November 2012).

Clearly, both far left and far right parties build on socialism and nationalism ideologies, respectively. Denmark is also a country where globalization tendencies and political uncertainties introduce 'political consumerism', with increased division between proponents and opponents of cosmopolitanism in the society (Andersen and Tobiasen, 2011: 203-204). Such political division empowered earlier marginal parties. The same political transformation also empowers ethnic communities. People have now a representative voice through leftist parties as well as the increasing number of empowered younger members of the community. Such representatives articulate and take political positions in the parliament and in the ranks of numerous political parties. Consequently, the earlier widespread naivety, in terms of not knowing other cultures and religions, particularly Islam, has declined. Currently, there are increasing calls for dialogue and coexistence:

Conclusion

Interest in socio-cultural divergence and exclusion was central to the rise and justification of populism in Denmark. Drawing on qualitative interviews and focus groups composed of members of ethnic communities in Denmark, this chapter argued that the socio-political exploitation of culture represented the means to achieving strategic political goals rather than the end. Though the public social and political discourse emphasized cultural distinction, it was the opportunity to question existing 'cultural symbolic constitution' (Hobsbawm, 1993:4) that provided spaces for community articulation and self-realization. With hyphenated identities and vibrant transnational connections, ethnic communities continuously reinvent and reimagine. To conceptualize this process requires critical analysis recognizing the potential of such communities, particularly their capabilities to access and create political spaces in ontologically nation-state centric societies.

For about a decade, anti-ethnic community populism polarized the Danish society. Combined national and international pressure as well as major social and economic events hindered such tendencies in taking root. Initially, ethnic communities played marginal roles, but members of the younger generations have gradually acquired diverse forms of capital and sought political influence. Apart from the increased controversy and division in the society, the top-down policy prioritization generated a bottom-up political mobilization both among native Danes and also among ethnic communities.

The rise of populism in Denmark led to significant changes both at the macro national level and also at the micro community level. For instance, though cultural tensions persist, many communities currently seem empowered in the transformed Danish political landscape. Similarly, previously marginal political parties at the far left and right have acquired influence and now aim directly to govern the country to a certain extent. On their part, ethnic communities also discovered that political participation is vital for achieving tangible change in the society. Though the communities remain marginal, conditions have improved as more people with the capability of maintaining transnational connections engage in political activism. So far, the norm of the traditional public debate, policy-making and research has focused on what others, both from instigators of exclusion and their adversaries, can do in relation to ethnic communities. This means less space for the transnational community to make choices and hold the agency that would allow it to navigate between community self-appraisal and a politically instigated clash of civilizations.

Bibliography

Aarts, Kees and Jaques, Thomassen (2008) 'Dutch Voters and the Changing Party Space 1989–2006', *Acta Politica* 43(2–3): 203–234.

Adam, Husein (1991) "Somalia: militarism, warlordism or democracy?" *Review of African Political Economy*, 19 (54):11-26.

Adams, Richard and Page, John (2005) "Do international migration and remittances reduce poverty in developing countries?" *World Development*, 33(10):1645–1669.

Adjiedj, Bakas (2009) *World Megatrends: Towards the Renewal of Humanity*. Oxford, UK.

Afrax, Mohamed (2010) "Towards a culture for peace, Poetry, Drama and Music in Somali society" *Accord*, Issue 21:72-74.

Afrax, Momahed (2000): Somali Theatre, Unpublished Doctoral Thesis, University of London

Ahmed, Ali (1995) (Ed.) *The invention of Somalia*. The Red Sea Press.

Ahmed, Ali (1996) *Daybreak is near-Literature, clans and the nation state in Somalia*, Red Sea Press

Ahmed, Shamima and David, Potter (2006) *NGOs in International Politics*. Kumarian Press.

Akkerman, Tjitske (2012) "Comparing Radical Right Parties in Government: Imimmigration and Integration Policies in Nine Countries (1996–2010)", *West European Politics* 35 (3) 511-529.

Akpınar, Pınar (2013) 'Turkey's Peacebuilding in Somalia: The Limits of Humanitarian Diplomacy', Special Issue: Turkey's Rise and the West: Conceptual Lenses and Actors, *Turkish Studies*, 14(4):735-757.

Ali, Degan and Kirsten, Gelsdorf (2012) "Risk-averse to risk-willing: Learning from the 2011 Somalia cash response" *Global Food Security*, No. 1:57–63.

Alpers, Edward (2014) *The Indian Ocean in World History*. Oxford University Press.

Al-sharmani, Mulki (2007) "Diasporic Somalis in Cairo: The poetics and practices of Soomaalinimo" in Kusow Abdi and Stephanie R. Bjork (eds.) From Mogadishu to Dixon, The Somali Diaspora in a global context. The Red Sea Press.

Anders Linde-Laursen (2007) "Is Something Rotten in the State of Denmark?-The Muhammad Cartoons and Danish Political Culture", *Contemporary Islam* 1: 265–274.

Andersen Jørgen Goul (2011) 'Vellykket Integration Integration: En succes som ingen ville tage æren for (Successful Integration Integration: A success that no one would take credit for)', *Information* 10 October p. 6, Viewed 1 October 2012, Infomedia.

Andersen Jørgen Goul and Mette Tobiasen (2011) "Who are these political consumers anyway? Survey evidence from Denmark" in (eds.) Michele Micheletti et al. *Politics, Products, and Markets: Exploring Political Consumerism*. Transaction Publishers.

Anderson Jon, Adey Peter and Bevan Paul (2010) 'Positioning place: Polylogic Approaches to Research Methodology', *Qualitative Research* 10: 589-604.

Anderson, B.; Sharma N. and Wright C. 2012. "We are all foreigners": No Borders as a Practical Political Project. In: Nyers P and Rygiel K (eds.) *Citizenship, Migrant Activism and the Politics of Movement* (Oxon: Routledge) pp.73-91.

Anderson, Benedict (2006) *Imagined Communities: Reflections on the Origin and Spread of Nationalism*. London: Verso.

Andreasson, Stefan (2011) "Africa's prospects and South Africa's leadership potential in the emerging markets century" *Third World Quarterly*, Vol. 32, No. 6, 2011, pp 1165–1181.

Anter, Andreas (2014) *Max Weber's Theory of the Modern State: Origins, Structure and Significance*. UK: Palgrave Macmillan.

Anthias, Floya (1998) Evaluating "Diaspora": Beyond Ethnicity. *Sociology* 32(3): 557-80.

Antonio, Gramsci (1971) "Intellectuals and Hegemony": *Prison Notebooks*. New York: International Publishers.

Appadurai, Arjun (1996) *Modernity at Large: Cultural Dimensions of Globalization*. Minnesota: University of Minnesota Press.

Appadurai, Arjun (2001) "Grassroots Globalization and the Research Imagination." In *Globalization* ed. Arjun, Appadurai, 1–21. Durham, NC: Duke University Press.

Appadurai, Arjun (2013) *The future as cultural fact: Essays on the global condition*. London: Verso.

Aradau, Claudia and van Munster, Rens (2008) "Insuring Terrorism, Assuring Subjects, Ensuring Normality: The Politics of Risk after 9/11", *Alternatives*, 33(2):191-210.

Arendt, Hannah (1970). On Violence, New York: Harcourt.

Bakhtin, Mikhail (1986) *Speech Genres & Other Late Essays*. Austin: University of Texas.

Bapat, Navin (2011) "Perspectives on Terrorism", *Journal of Peace Research*, 48(3):303-318.

Barnes, Cedric (2007) "The Somali Youth League, Ethiopian Somalis and the Greater Somalia Idea c.1946–48". *Journal of Eastern African Studies*, 1, No. 2:277-291

Barry, Sautman and Yan, Hairong (2009) "African perspectives on China–Africa links", *The China Quarterly*, 199: 728-759.

Basch, Linda, Nina Glick Schiller, and Cristina Szanton Blanc (eds.) 1994. *Nations Unbound Transnational Projects, Postcolonial*

Predicaments and De-territorialised Nation-States. Langhorne: Gordon and Breach.

Bassel, Leah (2007) "Refugee women and la République: participation in the French public sphere", *Parliamentary Affairs*, 60 (3): 467-481.

Bauböck Rainer and Thomas Faist (2010) (eds.) "Transnational and Transnationalism: Concepts, Theories and Methods" Amsterdam University Press.

Bauböck, Rainer (2009) "The rights and duties of external citizenship" *Citizenship studies*, 13(5):475-499.

Benhabib Seyla (2002) *The Claims of Culture: Equality and Diversity in the Global Era*. New Jersey: Princeton University Press.

Bloch, Alice (2000) "Refugee settlement in Britain: the impact of policy on participation" *Journal of Ethnic and Migration studies*, 26 (1):75-88.

Bonner, Michael (2005) "Poverty and Economics in the Qur'an" *The Journal of interdisciplinary history*, 35, No. 3: 391-406.

Bottomore, Thomas (1991) *Citizenship and Social Class*. Pluto Press.

Bourdieu, Pierre (1977) *Outline of a Theory of Practice*. Cambridge: Cambridge University Press.

Bourdieu, Pierre (1993) *The Field of Cultural Production: Essays on Art and Literature*. Cambridge: Polity Press.

Bourdieu, Pierre (1998) *Acts of Resistance: Against the Tyranny of the Market*, trans. R. Nice. New York: The New Press.

Bourdieu, Pierre (2000) *Pascalian Meditations*. Verso: Standford University Press.

Bourdieu, Pierre (2015) *Distinction: A Social Critique of the Judgement of Taste*. Routledge.

Bourdieu, Pierre (ed.) (1986) 'The forms of Capital' in J G Richardson *Handbook of Theory and Research for the Sociology of Education*. New York: Greenwood Press.

Boyle, Mark and Rob Kitchin (2014) "Diaspora centred development: Current practice, Critical commentaries and Research priorities" in S. Sahoo and P. Pattanaik (eds.), Global Diasporas and Development: Socioeconomic, cultural and policy Perspectives. India: Springer.

Bratton, Michael (1989) "The Politics of Government-NGO Relations in Africa", *World Development*, No. 17, 4: 569–587.

Bratton, Michael (1989) Beyond the State: Civil Society and Associational Life in Africa, Review article , *World Politics*, Vol. 41, No. 3 (Apr., 1989), pp. 407-430.

Breslin, Shaun (2013) "China and the global order: Signaling threat or friendship?", International Affairs, Special Issue: Negotiating the rise of new powers, 89 (3):615–634.

Breslin, Shaun and Ion Taylor (2008) "Explaining the rise of 'human rights' in analyses of Sino-African relations", *Review of African Political Economy*, 35 (1), pp. 59-71.

Brodmann, Stefanie and Javier, Polavieja (2011) 'Immigrants in Denmark: Access to Employment, Class Attainment and Earnings in a High-Skilled Economy', *International Migration* 49(1):58-90

Brynjolfsson, Erik; Andrew McAfee, and Michael Spence. "New World Order: Labor, Capital, and Ideas in the Power Law Economy". *Foreign Affairs*, July/August 2014.

Buckley-Zistel, Susanne (2006) "Dividing and uniting: The use of citizenship discourses in conflict and reconciliation in Rwanda", *Global Society*, 20(1), 101-113.

Calhoun, Craig (1993) 'Civil Society and the Public Sphere', *Public Culture* 5(2): 267–80.

Cassanelli, Lee (2009) 'The Partition of Knowledge in Somali Studies: Reflections on Somalia's Fragmented Intellectual Heritage". *An International Journal of Somali Studies*, No. 9,

(2009): *Article 2. Available at: http://digitalcommons.macalester.edu /bildhaan/vol9/iss1/2*

Cassanelli, Lee and Farah Abdikadir (2007) "Somalia: Education in Transition", *Bildhaan* Vol. 7

Cassanelli, Lee (1982) *The Shaping of Somali Society: Reconstructing the His-tory of a Pastoral People, 1600-1900.* Philadelphia: Univ. Penn. Press.

Castells, Manuel (2001) *The Internet Galaxy: Reflections on the Internet, Business, and Society.* Oxford: Oxford University Press.

Chabane, Djamel (2008) The Structure of 'umran al-'alam of Ibn Khaldun. Special Issue: The Worlds of Ibn-Khaldun. *The Journal of North African Studies* 13 (3): 331-349.

Chafer, Tony (2002) *The end of empire in French West Africa: France's successful d*

Chariandy, David (2006) Post-colonial Diasporas. In: Post-colonial text, 2(1). Available at: http://postcolonial.org/index.php/pct/article/view/440/159 (Accessed 18 December 2014)

Cheater, Angela and Rudo Gaidzanwa (1996) "Citizenship in neo-patrilineal states: gender and mobility in Southern Africa", *Journal of Southern African Studies*, 22 (2):189-200.

Chimmi, Sam (2012) "Global Capitalism and Global Democracy" in (eds.) Danielle Arhibugi, Mathias Koenig-Archibugi and Raffaele Marchetti *Global Democracy: Normative and Empirical Perspectives.* Cambridge: Cambridge University Press.

Christiansen, Connie (2011) 'Contesting Visibilities: Sartorial Strategies Among Muslim Women in Danish Media', *Journal of Intercultural Studies* 32 (4: 335-353.

Clarke, John (2005) "New Labour's citizens: Activated, Empowered, Responsibilized, abandoned?", *Critical social policy*, 25(4):447-463.

Cohen, Robert (1996) "Diaspora and the nation state: From victims to challengers" *International affairs*, 72 (1):507- 520).

Collier, Poul "It's Lonely Being No. , Is there Any Hope for Somalia?" Foreign Policy, June 2012

Contini, Paolo (1969) "The Somali Republic: an experiment in legal integration" Routledge Taylor.

Cox, Robert and Timothy Sinclair (2012) Approaches to World Order. Cambridge: Cambridge University Press.

Creswell, John (2009) *Research design: Qualitative, Quantitative, and Mixed Methods Approaches*. Thousand Islands, CA: SAGE Publications Inc.

Cunningham, Hilary (2000) "The Ethnography of Transnational Social Activism: Understanding the Global as Local Practice." American Ethnologist 26 (3): 583– 604.

Dagne, Theodore (2002) "Africa and the War on Terrorism: The Case of Somalia", *Mediterranean Quarterly*, 13 (4):62-73.

Dallmayr, Fred (2001) "Resisting Totalizing Uniformity: Marin Heidegger on the Macht and Machenschaft.", in Fred Dallmayr, *Achieving Our World: Toward a Global and Plural*, Lanham, MD: Rowman and Littlefield, 2001.

Dallmayr, Fred (2001). *Achieving our world: toward a global and plural democracy*. Rowman & Littlefield.

Dasgupta, Partha (2005) "Economics of social capital", *Economic Record*, 81(1):2-21.

De Tocqueville, Alex 2004) *Democracy in America* (A. Goldhammer, Trans. The library of America; 147). New York: Library of America.

Délano, Alexandra (2011) *Mexico and its Diaspora in the United States: Policies of Emigration since 1848,* Cambridge: Cambridge University Press.

Diamond, Larry (2008) "The rule of law versus the big man", *Journal of Democracy*, 19(2):138-149.

Durkheim, Emil (1993) *The Division of Labour in Society* (George Simpson). New York: Macmillan.
ecolonization. Berg.
Eggebø, Helga (2010) "The problem of dependency: immigration, gender, and the welfare state". *Social Politics: International Studies in Gender, State & Society*, 17(3): 295-322.
Ehrenberg, John (1999) *Civil Society*. New York: New York University Press.
El-Gabalawi, Nabila (2010) *Peace building in Application of the Work of Ngos in Conflict Areas*. Germany. Grin Verlag.
Elmi, Afyare, and Abdullahi, Barise (2006) "The Somali Conflict: Root causes, obstacles, and peace-building strategies". *African Security Review*, 15 (1):32-54.
Ezzat, Hebba (2005) "Beyond Methodological Modernism: Towards a Multicultural Paradigm Shift in the Social Sciences." *Global Civil Society* edited by Helmut Anhelier et al, London: Sage.
Faist, Thomas (2000) Transnationalization in International Migration: Implications for the study of Citizenship and Culture. *Ethnic and Racial Studies* 23(2):189-222.
Falk, Richard (2012) The Promise and Perils of Global Democracy' in (eds.) Danielle Arhibugi, Mathias Koenig-Archibugi and Raffaele Marchetti *Global Democracy: Normative and Empirical Perspectives*. Cambridge: Cambridge University Press.
Fangen, Katrine (2007) "Breaking up the Different Constituting Parts of Ethnicity: The Case of Young Somalis in Norway", *Acta Sociologica*, 50(4): 401–414.
Farah, Abdulkadir and Ali Yusuf "Hadraawi"s peace journey (Socdaalka nabadda) reaches Aarhus, Denmark" (November 30, 2004):, [WWW Document] URL http://www.hiiraan.ca/2003/nov03/hadrawi_den.htm?ID=46923, [30/03/2004

Farah, Ahmed and Iain, Lewis (1993) Somalia: the roots of reconciliation Peace making endeavours of contemporary lineage leaders; a survey of grassroots peace conferences in `Somaliland'. Report by Action Aid (UK).

Farah, Osman A. (2012) *Transnationalism and Civic Engagement: Diasporic Formation and Mobilization in Denmark and the UAE.* London: Adonis & Abbey Publishers.

Feature report (1992) "Starvation and terror in Somalia." *Foreign Policy Bulletin.* No. 3(2):22-31 Cambridge University Press.

Ferguson, James (2006) *Global Shadows: Africa in the Neoliberal World Order.* London: Duke University Press.

Findley, Michael and Joseph Young (2012) "Terrorism and civil war: A spatial and temporal approach to a conceptual problem", *Perspectives on Politics*, 10(02): 285-305.

Fiona, Adamson (2013) "Mechanisms of Diaspora mobilization and the Trans-nationalization of Civil war" in Jeffrey T. Checke (ed.), Transnational Dynamics of Civil War. Cambridge: Cambridge University Press.

Firebaugh, Glenn (2006) *The New Geography of Global Income Inequality.* USA: Harvard college.

Fish, Jonathan (2005) *Defending the Durkheimian Tradition: Religion, Emotion and Morality.* Ashgate Publishing.

Fituni, Leonid (2014) "From Boulders to Ashlars- BRICS of a New World Order: Hierarchies of Power and Degrees of Freedom in the merging World System of the Twenty-first Century" in Li Xing (ed.) *The BRICS and Beyond- The International Political Economy of the Emergence of a New World Order*, London: Ashgate.

FitzGerald, David (2012) A comparativist manifesto for international migration studies. *Ethnic and Racial Studies*, 35(10):1725-1740.

Fokuyama, Francis (2014) *Political Order and Political Decay: From the Industrial Revolution to the globalization of democracy.* New York: Macmillan.

Foucault, Michel (1980) *Power/knowledge: Selected interviews and other writings 1972-1977.* Brighton: Harvester Press (109-133).

Foucault, Michel (1982) Afterword: The Subject and Power. In Dreyfus HL and Rabinow P (eds.) *Michel Foucault: Beyond Structuralism and Hermeneutics.* Brighton: The Harvester Press. pp. 208–26.

Fraser, Nancy (2007) "Transnational Public Sphere: Transnationalizing the Public Sphere: On the Legitimacy and Efficacy of Public Opinion in a Post-Westphalian World. Theory", Culture, Society, 24(4): 7-30.

Fraser, Nancy (2014) "Publicity, Subjection, and Critique: A Reply to my Critics" in Nancy Fraser et al. (ed.) Kate Nash *Transnationalizing the Public Sphere.* Cambridge: Polity Press.

Gann, Lewis and Duignan, Peter (1975) (Ed) Colonialism in Africa 1870-1960: The economics of colonialism. Vail-Ballou Press: New York.

Ghannushi, Rashid (1993) *"Xuququl muwadina: Xuquq geyrul muslimün fi-mujtamac-alislami"* (Citizenship rights: the rights of non-Muslims in Muslim society. International Institute for Islamic thinking, London.

Giri, Ananta (2006) Creative Social Research: Rethinking Theories and Methods and the Calling of an Ontological Epistemology of Participation. *Dialectical Anthropology* 30: 227–71.

Giri, Ananta (2000) "Rethinking human well-being: a dialogue with Amartya Sen", *Journal of International Development,* 12(7): 1003.

Giri, Ananta (2012) *Knowledge and Human Liberation: Towards Planetary Realizations.* London: Anthem Press.

Givens, Terri (2005) *Voting Radical Right in Western Europe.* Cambridge UK: Cambridge University Press.

Gleissner, John (2010) *Prison and Slavery - A Surprising Comparison.* USA: Outskirts Press.

Goldberg, Allan (2008) Introduction of Emile Durkheim's "Anti-Semitism and Social Crisis". *Sociological Theory* 26 (4): 299-323).

Goldman, Michael. (2005). *Imperial Nature: The World Bank and Struggles for Social Justice in the Age of Globalization.* New Haven, CT and London: Yale University Press.

Granovetter, Mark (1973) The strength of weak ties. *American Journal of Sociology,* 78 (6): 1360-1380.

Green-Pedersen Christoffer and Krogstrup Odmalm (2008) 'Immigration as a political issue in Denmark and Sweden', *European Journal of Political Research, 47(5):610–634*

Gregory, Chin and Fahimul, Quadir (2012) "Introduction: Rising States, Rising Donors and the Global Aid Regime", *Cambridge Review of International Affairs,* 25 (4): 493-506.

Gundel, Joakim (2006) "The predicament of the 'Oday'. The role of traditional structures in security, rights, law and development in Somalia." Final Report. Danish Refugee Council and Novib-Oxfam, Nairobi.

Gundelach Peter (2010) 'Democracy and denomination: democratic values among Muslim minorities and the majority population in Denmark', *Ethnic and Racial Studies* 33(3): 426-450.

Haan, Nicholas; Devereux, Stephen and Maxwell, Daniel (2012) "Global implications of Somalia 2011 for famine prevention, mitigation and response " *Global Food Security,* No. 1: 74–79.

Habermas, Jürgen (1979) *Communication and the Evolution of Society.* Translated by T McCarthy. Boston.

Habermas, Jürgen (2009) *Between Facts and Norms*. UK: Polity Press.

Habermas, Jürgen (1990) *Moral Consciousness and Communicative Action*. Cambridge: Polity Press.

Habermas, Jürgen (1998) 'Beyond the nation state?', Peace Review: A Journal of Social Justice Special Issue: National Self-Determination, 10/2: 235-239.

Habermas, Jürgen. 1991. *The Structural Transformation of the Public Sphere: An Inquiry into a Category of Bourgeois Society*. Cambridge, Mass.: MIT Press.

Hagmann, Tobias and Hoehne, Markus (2009) "Failures of the state failure debate: Evidence from the Somali territories." *Journal of international development*, 21 (1):42–57

Halabi, Yakub (2009) *US Foreign Policy in the Middle East: From Crises to Change*. England: Ashgate.

Hall, Stuart (1990) 'Cultural Identity and Diaspora' in (ed.) Jonathan R *Identity, Community, Culture, Difference*. London: Lawrence and Wishart.

Halliday, Fred (2001) "The Romance of Non-State Actors," in *Non-State Actors in World Politics* edited by D. Josselin and W. Wallace, London: Palgrave, pp. 21–37.

Hammond, Laura. (2013). 'Somalia rising: things are starting to change for the world's longest failed state', *Journal of Eastern African Studies*, 7/1:183-193

Hannerz, Ulf (2002) *Transnational connections: Culture, people, places*. Taylor & Francis US.

Hannerz, Ulf (2003) "Being There . . . and There . . . and There! Reflections on Multisite Ethnography", Ethnography, 4(2): 201–16.

Hanusch, Marek (2012) "African Perspectives on China-Africa: Modelling Popular Perceptions and their Economic and

Political Determinants", *Oxford Development Studies*, 40 (4):492-516.

Harvey, David (2000) *Spaces of Hope*. Edinburgh: Edinburgh University Press.

Hegel, G.W.F. (1821/1991) *Elements of the Philosophy of Right*, trans. H.B. Nisbett, ed. and introd. A.W. Wood. Cambridge: Cambridge University Press.

Hepner Tricia Redeker (2003) Religion, Nationalism, and Transnational Civil Society in the Eritrean Diaspora, *Identities: Global Studies in Culture and Power*, 10(3)269-293.

Herb, Michael (2009) A Nation of Bureaucrats: Political Participation and Economic Diversification in Kuwait and the UnitedArab Emirates. *International Journal of Middle East Studies*, 41: 375–395.

Herbst, Jeffrey (2014) *States and Power in Africa: Comparative Lessons in Authority and Control: Comparative Lessons in Authority and Control*. Princeton University Press.

Hertz, Noreena (2004) 'Corporations on the Front Line.' *Corporate Governance: An International Review*, 12(2):202–209.

Hervik, Peter and Rytter M (2004) 'Med ägteskab i Focus' In: *Ægtefællesammenføring i Danmark*. Copenhagen: Institute for Human Rights, pp.131–160.

Hervik, Peter (2012) 'Ending tolerance as a solution to incompatibility: The Danish crisis of multiculturalism', *European Journal of Cultural Studies* 15: 211.

Hobsbawm, Eric (1983) 'Introduction: Inventing Traditions' in (eds.) Eric Hobsbawm and Terence Ranger *The Invention of Tradition*. Cambridge: Cambridge University Press.

Hobsbawm, Eric (2012) *Nations and nationalism since 1780: Programme, myth, reality*. Cambridge University Press.

Holub, Renate (1992) Antonio Gramsci: Beyond Marxism and Post-modernism, Routledge

Horowitz, Donald (1985) *Ethnic Groups in Conflict*. Berkeley: University of California Press.

Horst Cindy (2004) "Money and mobility: transnational livelihood strategies of the Somali diaspora", Global Migration perspectives, nr. 9 October 2004, *International migration* (GCIM)

Hugo, Graeme (2004) International Migration in the Asia-Pacific Region: Emerging Trends and Issues. In: Massey DS and Taylor JE (eds.) *International Migration Prospects and Policies in a Global Market* (Oxford: Oxford University Press, 2004) pp.77–104.

Huntington, Samuel (1993) "The Clash of Civilizations The clash of civilizations?", *Foreign Affairs* Summer 72 (3).

Huntington, Samuel. *Political Order in Changing Societies*. New Haven and London: Yale University Press, 1968.

Hussain, Yasmin, and Paul Bagguley (2005) "Citizenship, Ethnicity and Identity British Pakistanis after the 2001 'Riots'", *Sociology*, 39(3): 407-425.

Ibn Khaldun (1981) *AlMuqaddimah*. Beirut: Dar al-Qalam, trans.

Ibn Khaldun, A.R. (1979), Muqaddimah Ibn Khaldun, Daru Nahdatu Mysr, Cairo.

Jakobsen, Linda (2009) "China's diplomacy toward Africa: Drivers and Constraints", *International Relations of the Asia-Pacific*, 9(3):403-33.

Jenkins, Richard (2013) *Pierre Bourdieu*. Routledge.

Jensen Sune (2011) 'Othering, Identity formation and Agency', *Qualitative studies*, 2(2), 63-78.

Jones, Branwen (2008) "The global political economy of social crisis: Towards a critique of the 'failed state' ideology." *Review of International Political Economy*, 15 (2)180-205.

Jones, Stephanie (2012) *BRICs and Beyond: Lessons on Emerging Markets*. London: Wiley

Kadri, Ali (2014) *Dynamics of Accumulation by Wars of Encroachment*. Anthem Press.

Kaldor, Mary; Helmut, Anheier and Marlies, Glasius (2003) *Global civil society*. Cambridge: Polity.

Kanna, Ahmed (2011) *Dubai, the City as Corporation*. Minnesota: University of Minnesota Press.

Kapchitz, Georgi (2010) "Reports on Somalia" I, II, III and IV (www.wardheernews.com)

Kapteijns, Lidwien (2004) "Government Qadis and Child Marriage in Aden: Ethnography in the Aden Archives.". *International Journal of African Historical Studies*, 37(3): 401-434.

Kasim, Mohamed. (1995). 'Aspects of Banadir cultural history: The case of the Bravan Ulama' in (eds.) The Invention of Somalia, Ali Jimale Ahmed. New Jersey: Red Sea Press.

Katz, Richard and Mair Peter (2012) Parties, interest groups and cartels: A comment *Party Politics* 2012 18: 107

Keck, Margaret and Sikkink, Kathryn (1998) *Activists beyond borders: Advocacy networks in International politics*. Cornell University.

Keohane, Robert and Joseph Nye (2000) "Globalization: What's new? What's not?(And so what?)." *Foreign policy*, 104-119.

Keohane, Robert and Joseph Nye (2011) *Power and interdependence*. Longman.

Keohane, Robert and Joseph, Nye (1972) *Transnational Relations and World Politics*. Cambridge: Harvard University Press.

Khaldor, Mary (2012) *New and Old Wars: Organized Violence in a Global Era*. London: Polity Press.

Kharas, Homi and Rogerson, Andrew (2007) *Horizon 2025: creative destruction in the aid industry, agenda for peace and development*. Earthscan.

Kivisto, Peter and Thomas, Faist (2010) *Beyond a Border: The Causes and Consequences of Contemporary Immigration*. London, UK: Sage publications

Kornegay, Francis and Muller Narnia (2013) (eds.) *Laying the BRICS of a New Global Order: From Yekaterinburg 2009 to eThekwini*

Kraxberger, Brennan (2005) "Strangers, indigenes and settlers: contested geographies of citizenship in Nigeria", *Space and polity*, 9(1):9-27.

Kretzmer, David; Eckart Klein and Eckart Klein (2002) *The concept of human dignity in human rights discourse*. The Hague: Kluwer Law International.

Kühle, Lene and Lasse Lindekilde (2012) 'Radicalisation and the Limits of Tolerance: A Danish Case-Study', *Journal of Ethnic and Migration Studies* 38 (10): 1607-1623.

Kundnani, Arun (2007) *The end of tolerance: racism in 21st century Britain*. Pluto Press.

Kusow, Abdi (2003) Beyond Indigenous Authenticity: Reflections on the Insider/Outsider Debate in Immigration Research. *Symbolic Interaction* 26 (4): 591–599.

Kusow, Abdi (2004) *Contested Narratives and the Crisis of the Nation-State in Somalia: A prolegomenon. Putting the Cart before the Horse: Contested Nationalism and the Crisis of the Nation-state in Somalia*. Red Sea Press.

Lacher, Wolfram (2008) "The Political Economy of the Saharan Threat", *Security Dialogue*, 39(4):383-405.

Laitin, David and Said Samatar (1987) *Somalia: nation in search of a state*. Westview Pr.

Lambert, David and Alan Lester (2006) (eds.) *Colonial Lives Across the British Empire: Imperial Careering in the Long Nineteen Century*. Cambridge: Cambridge University Press.

Lang, Sabine (2013) *NGOs, Society and the Public Sphere*. Cambridge: Cambridge University Press.

Le Sage, Andre (2005) *Stateless Justice in Somalia: Formal and informal rule of law initiatives*. Centre for Humanitarian Dialogue.

Lears, Jackson "The Concept of cultural hegemony: problems and possibilities" in (eds.) James Martin, Antonio Gramsci: Contemporary applications. New York: Routledge.

Leeson, Peter (2006) Better Off Stateless: Somalia Before and After Government Collapse, SSRN Working Paper Series.

Levitt, Peggy and Nina Glick-Schiller, 2004. Conceptualizing Simultaneity: A Transnational Social Field Perspective on Society. *International Migration Review*, 38:1002-39.

Lewis, David (2001) "Civil society in non-Western contexts: reflections on the 'usefulness' of a concept. Civil Society Working Paper series, 13. Centre for Civil Society, London School of Economics and Political Science, London, UK. ISBN 0753013789

Lewis, Ian (1999) *A Pastoral Democracy: a study of pastoralism and politics among the northern Somali of the Horn of Africa*. James Currey Publishers.

Lindekilde, Lasse (2010) 'Soft Repression and Mobilization: The case of Transnational Activism of Danish Muslims during the Cartoon Controversy', *International Journal of Middle East Studies* 42(3):451–469.

Little, David (2003). *Somalia: Economy without state*. Indiana University Press.

Lobell, Steven & Mauceri Philip (2004) *Ethnic conflict and international politics: explaining diffusion*, Palgrave

Lyons, Michal, Brown, Alison and Zhigang, Li (2012) "In the Dragon's Den: African traders in Guangzhou", *Journal of Ethnic and Migration Studies*, 38(5):869-888.

Lyons, Michel and Brown, Alison (2010) "Has Mercantilism reduced Urban Poverty in SSA? Perception of Boom, Bust, and the China-Africa trade in Lomé and Bamako", *World Development* 38 (5):771-782.

Mack Michael (2001) "The metaphysics of eating: Jewish dietary law and Hegel's social theory", *Philosophy Social Criticism,* 27: 59

Mahdavi, Pardis (2011) *Gridlock: Labor, Migration, and Human Trafficking in Dubai.* Stanford: Stanford University Press.

Malik Maleiha (ed.) (2013) *Anti-Muslim Prejudice: Past and Present.* London: Routledge.

Mamdani, Mahmood (2002) *When Victims Become Killers: Colonialism, Nativism and the Genocide in Rwanda.* New Jersey: Princeton University Press.

Mamdani, Mahmood (2007) *Scholars in the Marketplace: The Dilemmas of Neo-liberal Reform at Makerere University, 1989-2005.* African Books Collective.

Marcus, George (1995) "Ethnography in/of the World System: The Emergence of Multi-Sited Ethnography", *Annual Review of Anthropology,* 24:95–117.

Maren, Michael (2009) *The Road to Hell.* New York: Free Press.

Marpil, J (2009) The Place of Sacrifice: Qurbani and Transnational Circuits among Bangladeshis in Lisbon. *Analise Social* 44(190): 71-103.

Martin, Bradford (2003) *Muslim Brotherhoods in Nineteenth-Century Africa.* Cambridge: Cambridge University Press.

Mazrui, Ali (1976) Soldiers as Traditionalizers: Military Rule and the Re-Africanization of Africa, *World Politics,* 28 (2):246-27.

Mazrui, Ali (1993) The introduction. In: Mazrui A. (eds.) *General history of Africa: Africa since 1935,* UNESCO 1-23.

Mazrui, Ali (1978) *Political Values and the Educated Class in Africa.* Berkeley, CA: University of California.

Mazrui, Ali (1986) *The political sociology of the English language*, Hague

Menkhaus, Ken (2000) "Traditional Conflict Management in Contemporary Somalia" in *Traditional Cures for Modern Conflicts: African Conflict "Medicine"* edited by William Zartman. Colorado: Lynne Rienner Publishers.

Menkhaus, Ken (2007) "The crises in Somalia: Tragedy in five acts." *African Affairs*, 106 (204):357–390.

Menkhaus, Ken (2012) "No access: Critical bottlenecks in the 2011 Somali famine". *Global Food Security*, No. 1: 29–35.

Merry, Sally (2006) "Transnational Human Rights and Local Activism: Mapping the Middle." *American Anthropologist*, 108 (1):38–51.

Mewes Jan and Steffen Mau (2013) "Globalization, socio-economic status and welfare chauvinism: European perspectives on attitudes toward the exclusion", *International Journal of Comparative Sociology*, 54(3): 228-245.

Mezzetti, Petra; Saggiomo, Valeria; Pirkkalainen, Päivi; Guglielmo, Matteo (2010) "Engagement dynamics between diasporas and settlement country institutions : Somalis in Italy and Finland". University of Jyväskylä, Diaspeace Project. - (Diaspeace working paper. ISSN 1798-1689; No. 6.

Modi, Renu (2014) "BRICS and Bilaterals: Synergies and Contestations" in Li Xing (ed.)*The BRICS and Beyond- The International Political Economy of the Emergence of a New World Order*. London: Ashgate.

Mohamoud, Abdullah (2005) *State Collapse and Post-Conflict Development in Africa: The Case of Somalia*, Purdue University Press

Mohan, Giles (2007) "Participatory development: from epistemological reversals to active citizenship", *Geography Compass*, 1(4): 779-796.

Mouritsen Per and Tore Olsen (2013) 'Denmark between liberalism and nationalism', *Ethnic and Racial Studies*, 36(4):691-710.

Mueni, Muiu (2010) "Colonial and Postcolonial State and Development in Africa", *An International Quarterly*, 77(4):1311– 1338.

Mukhtar, Mohamed (1996) "The plight of the Agro-pastoral society of Somalia". *Review of African Political Economy*, 23 (70): 543-553.

Munck, Ronaldo, Carl Ulrik Schierup, and Raúl Delgado Wise (2011) "Migration, work, and citizenship in the new world order" *Globalizations*, 8(3):249-260.

Murithi, Tim (2012) "Towards the metamorphosis of the United Nations: a proposal for establishing global democracy" in Danielle Arhibugi, Mathias Koenig-Archibugi and Raffaele Marchetti (eds.) *Global Democracy: Normative and Empirical Perspectives*. Cambridge: Cambridge University Press.

Nilüfer, Gole (1996), *The forbidden Modern: Civlization and Veiling* (Michigan)

Nader, Lucia (2013) "Mismatch: why are human rights NGOs in emerging powers not emerging?" at www.opendemocracynet.com (accessed November 2014).

Nagel, Caroline and and Lynn Staeheli (2004) "Citizenship, identity and transnational migration: Arab immigrants to the United States", *Space and Polity*, 8 (1):3-23.

Naidu, Sanusha (2007) "The forum on China–Africa cooperation (FOCAC): what does the future hold?" *China Report*, 43(3):283–296.

Naufal, George and Ali Termos (2009) 'The Responsiveness of Remittances to the Oil Price: The Case of the GCC', Discussion Paper Series, IZA DP No. 4277 (Bonn: IZA, 2009).

Neilson, Brett and Rossiter, Net (2005) From Precarity to Precariousness and Back Again: Labour, Life and Unstable Networks. *Fibre culture Journal*, 5, http://five.fibreculturejournal.org/fcj-022-from-precarityto-precariousness-and-back-again-labour-life-and-unstable-networks/ (downloaded 10 April 2015).

Nielsen, Jørgen (2011) *Islam in Denmark: The Challenge of Diversity.* Maryland USA: Lexington books.

Nielsen, Jørgen (ed.) (2012) 'Setting the scene: Muslims in Denmark' in Jørgen S. Nielsen, *Islam in Denmark: The Challenge of Diversity.* Maryland: Lexington Books.

Njoh, Ambe (2006) *Tradition, Culture and Development in Africa: Historical Lessons for Modern development planning.* England UK: Ashgate publishing.

Nussbaum, Martha (2011) *Creating Capabilities: The Human Development Approach.* Harvard University Press.

Obiorah, Ndubisi (2007) "Who's Afraid of China", in Manji, Firoze and Marks, Stephen (eds.) *African Perspectives on China in Africa.* Nairobi: Fahamu.

Ostegard, Robert; Laremond, Recardo and Klauche, Fouad (2004). *Power, Politics, and the African Condition.* New Jersey: Africa World Press.

Paffenholz, Thania (2010) *Civil society and peacebuilding: a critical assessment.* Lynne Rienner Publishers.

Papastergiadis, Nikos (2000) *The Turbulence of Migration: Globalization, De-territorialization, and Hybridity.* Blackwell.

Patterson, Rubin (2006) "Transnationalism: Diaspora-homeland development", *Social Forces*, 84(4):1891–1907.

Peck, Malcolm (1986) *The United Arab Emirates: A Venture in Unity*. London: Westview Press.

Pedersen Karina (2012) 'The 2011 Danish Parliamentary Election: A Very New Government', *West European Politics*, 35(2): 415-424.

Pellerina, Hélène and Beverley, Mullings (2013) "The 'Diaspora option', migration and the changing political economy of development", *Review of International Political Economy*, 20(1): 89-120.

Pentikäinen Merja (2008) *Creating an Integrated Society and Recognizing Differences: The Role and Limits of Human Rights, with special reference to Europe*. Lapland: Lapland University Press.

Stearns, Peter (ed.) (2008) *Oxford Encyclopedia of the Modern World*. Oxford University Press.

Peutz, Nathalie, et al. (2006) "Embarking on an Anthropology of Removal", *Current Anthropology*, 47(2): 217-241.

Pickering Willaim (1975) *Durkheim on Religion: a Selection of Readings with Bibliographies*. Volume 1: Routledge.

Piles, Peter (1992) "Going it Alone", *Africa Report*, 37(1):58-61.

Poddar, Prem et al (2008) *A Historical Companion to Postcolonial Literatures: Continental Europe and its empires*, Edinburg University Press

Polanyi, Karl (1944, 1957) *The Great Transformation: the political and economic origins of our time*. Boston: Beacon Press.

Poulantzas, Nicos (2000) *State, power, socialism*. London: Verso.

Putnam, Robert (2000) *Bowling Alone: The Collapse and Revival of American Community*. New York: Simon and Schuster.

Putnam, Robert (1993) *Making Democracy Work: Civic traditions in modern Italy*. Princeton, NJ: Princeton University Press.

Reeskens, Tim and Oorschot van Wim (2012) 'Disentangling the 'New Liberal Dilemma': On the relation redistribution preferences and welfare chauvinism between general welfare', *International Journal of Comparative Sociology* 53(2): 120-139.

Richard, Falk (2003) *The Great Terror War.* New York: Olive Branch Press.

Riles, Annelise (2000) The Network Inside Out. Ann Arbor: University of Michigan Press.

Risse, Thomas (2013) (Ed.) *Governance without a state?: policies and politics in areas of limited statehood.* Columbia University Press.

Roche, Jeremy (1999) "Children: Rights, participation and citizenship", *Childhood*, 6(4), 475-493.

Roitman, Janet (2007) "The right to tax: economic citizenship in the Chad Basin", *Citizenship studies*, 11(2):187-209.

Rojecki, Andrew (20089 "Rhetorical Alchemy: American Exceptionalism and the War on Terror", *Political Communication*, 25(1):67-88

Rose, Fred (2000) *Coalitions across the class divide: Lessons from the labor, peace, and environmental movements.* Cornell University Press.

Rutherford, Kenneth (2008) *Humanitarianism under Fire: The US and UN Intervention in Somalia. USA*: Kumarian Press.

Rydgren, Jens and Ruth Patrick (2011) Voting for the radical right in Swedish municipalities: Social marginality and ethnic competition? *Scandinavian Political Studies*, 34(3): 202–225.

Rytter Mikkel (2011) "Money or Education? Improvement Strategies Among Pakistani Families in Denmark", *Journal of Ethnic and Migration Studies*, 37(2), 197-215.

Said, Edward (2001) 'The Clash of Ignorance' *The Nation* October 22.

Salehyan, Idean (2011) *Rebels without Borders: Transnational Insurgencies in World Politics.* New York: Cornell University Press.

Samatar, Abdi (1989) *The State and Rural Transformation in Northern Somalia, 1884-1986*, Wisconson Press

Samatar, Abdi (1993) "Structural Adjustment as Development Strategy? Bananas, Boom, and Poverty in Somalia", *Economic Geography*, 69 (1):25-43.

Samatar, Abdi (2008) "Somali reconstruction and local initiative: Amoud University" *World development"*, 29 (4):641-656.

Samatar, Abdi (1992) Destruction of State and Society in Somalia: Beyond the Tribal Convention, *The Journal of Modern African Studies*, 30(4):625-641.

Samatar, Ahmed (1988) *Socialist Somalia: Rhetoric and Reality*, London: Zed.

Samatar, Said (1979) *Poetry in Somali politics: the case of Sayyid Mahammad A'bdille Hassan*, Vol. 1

Sanfilippo, Marco (2010) "Chinese FDI to Africa: What Is the Nexus with Foreign Economic Cooperation?", *African Development Review*, 22(1):599–614.

Sautman, Barry and Hairong, Yan (2008) "The forest for the trees: Trade, investment and the China-in-Africa discourse", *Pacific Affairs*, 81(1):9-29.

Schierup, Carl-Ulrik, Aleksandra Ålund, and Branka Likić-Brborić (2014) Migration, Precarization and the Democratic Deficit in Global Governance. *International Migration*. doi: 10.1111/imig.12171

Schmidt Garbi (2011) 'Understanding and Approaching Muslim Visibilities: Lessons Learned from a Fieldwork-based Study of Muslims in Copenhagen', *Ethnic and Racial Studies*, 34 (7): 1216-1229.

Scholte, Jan (2000) *Globalization: A critical introduction* (Basingtoke: Palgrave, Macmillan)

Scott John and Gordon Marshall (2009) (eds.) *A Dictionary of Sociology*. Oxford: Oxford University Press.

Sefa Dei, George (2010) *Teaching Africa: Towards a Transgressive Pedagogy.* New York: Springer.

Sen, Amartya (2008) Violence, Identity and Poverty, *Journal of Peace Research*, 45 (5): 5-15.

Sen, Amartya (2007) *Identity and Violence: The illusion of Destiny.* India: Benguin Books.

Sen, Amartya (2000) "Consequential Evaluation and Practical Reason', *The Journal of Philosophy*, 97(9): 477-502.

Sen, Amartya (2009) *The Ideas of justice.* MA: Harvard University Press.

Sen, Amartya (2011) *The idea of justice.* Harvard University Press.

Sen, Amartya (2015) *Identity and Violence: The Illusion of Destiny.* Penguin.

Shain, Yossi (2000) "The Mexican-American diaspora's impact on Mexico", *Political Science Quarterly*, 114(4): 661-691.

Shaw, Timothy (2012) "Africa's Quest for Developmental States: 'Renaissance' for whom?" *Third World Quarterly*, 33 (5):837–851.

Shaw, Timothy (2014) "The BRICS and Beyond: New Global Order, Reorder and/or Disorder? Insights from "Global Governance" in Li Xing (ed.) The BRICS and Beyond- The International Political Economy of the Emergence of a New World Order. London: Ashgate.

Sheffer, Gabriel (2003) *Diaspora Politics: At Home Abroad.* Cambridge: Cambridge University Press.

Sheffer, Gabriel (1986) *Modern Diasporas in international relations.* Croom Helm.

Sheik-Abdi, Abdi (1977) "*Somali Nationalism: Its Origins and Future*" *The Journal of Modern African Studies*, 15(4): 657-665.

Shelley, Louise (2010) *Human perspective: A Global perspectives.* Cambridge: Cambridge University Press.

Shen, Simon (2009) "A constructed (un)reality on China's re-entry into Africa: The Chinese Online Community Perception of Africa (2006-2008)", *Journal of Modern African Studies*, 47(3):425-448.

Sidaway, James (2012) "Geographies of Development: New Maps, New Visions?" *The Professional Geographer*, 64(1):49–62.

Simmel, George (1971) "The Stranger" In *on Individuality and Social Forms*. (ed.) D Levine. Chicago: University of Chicago Press. PP. 143–49.

Six, Clemens (2009) "The Rise of Postcolonial States as Donors: a challenge to the development paradigm?", *Third World Quarterly*, 30(6):1103-1121.

Skoczylas, Tomasz and Adam Mrozowicki (2012) Review: The Precariat: the New Dangerous Class by Guy Standing. *Labor History* 53(4):588-589.

Smith, Anthony (1991) *National identity*. University of Nevada Press.

Smith, C. 2010. Go with the flow: labour power mobility and labour process theory. In: Thompson P and Smith C (eds.) *Working Life: Renewing Labour Process Analysis*. London: Palgrave, 269–96.

Smith, Graham (1999) Transnational Politics and the Politics of the Russian Diaspora. *Ethnic and Racial Studies*, 22(3):500-523.

Smith, Jackie (2001) "Globalizing Resistance: The Battle of Seattle and the Future of Social Movements." *Mobilization: An International Quarterly*, 6 (1): 1 – 19

Smith, Michael Peter, and Luis Eduardo Guarnizo (1998) *Transnationalism from Below*. New Jersey: Transaction Publishers.

Sniderman Paul et al. (2014) *Paradoxes of Liberal Democracy: Islam, Western Europe, and the Danish Cartoon Crises*. Princeton: Princeton University Press.

Sokefeld, Martin (2006) "Mobilizing in Transnational Space: A social movement approach to the formation of Diaspora", *Global networks*, 6(3):265-84.

Sorensen, Georg (1999) *Development in Fragile and failed states*, Political Science Department, Aarhus University, Denmark

Sornarayah, Muthucumaraswamy (2014) "The role of the BRICS in international law in a Multipolar world" in Vai Io Lo and Mary Hiscock (ed.)*The Rise of the BRICS in the Global Political Economy: Changing Paradigms?*. Edward Elgar Publishing: Cheltenham-UK.

Soysal, Yasmin (2000) "Citizenship and Identity: Living in diasporas in post-war Europe?", *Ethnic and Racial Studies*, 23(1):1-15.

Stalker, Peter (1998) (Ed.) "States of Disarray: The Social Effects of Globalization" United Nations research institute for development.

Standing, Guy (2011) *The Precariat: The New Dangerous Class*. New York: Bloomsbury Publications.

Stearns, Peter (ed.) (2008) *Oxford Encyclopedia of the Modern World*. Oxford: Oxford University Press.

Sterling, Jennifer (2008) "The Emperor Wore Cowboy Boots", *International Studies Perspectives*, 9(3):319-330.

Straziuso, Jason (2013) (AP)-Report: 260,000 Died in Somali Famine, (http://world.time.com/2013/04/29/report-260000-died-in-somali-famine/), 2013 accessed 30th April 2013).

Subrah, Manyam (1997) *The Career and Legend of Vasco da Gama*, Cambridge University Press, Cambridge

Subrah, Sanjay (1997) *The Career and Legend of Vasco da Gama*, Cambridge University Press, Cambridge

Suryadinata, Leo (2000) *Nationalism and Globalization: East and West.* Institute of South East Asian studies.

Suzuki, Shogo (2009) "Chinese Soft Power, Insecurity studies, Myopia and Fantasy", *Third World Quarterly*, 30(4):779-793.

Sylvanus Nina (2007) "The fabric of Africanity: Tracing the global Threads of Authenticity", *Anthropological Theory*, 7 (2):201-216.

Tarrow, Sidney (1994) *Power in movement: Social movements, collective action, and politics.* Cambridge: Cambridge University Press.

Tarrow, Sidney (1996) "Social Movements in Contentious Politics: A Review Article", *The American Political Science Review*, 90 (4):874-883.

Tarrow, Sidney (2005) *The new transnational activism.* Cambridge University Press.

Taylor, Charles (2011) Dilemmas and connections: Selected essays. Harvard University Press.

Taylor, Ion (2006) "China's oil diplomacy in Africa", *International Affairs*, 85 (5):937-959.

Taylor, Ion (2014) *Africa Rising: BRICS- Diversifying Dependence.* Rochester US: Boydell & Brewer

Tedler, Judith (1997). *Good government in topics.* Baltimore, MD: John Hopkins University Press.

Terterov, Marat (2006) *Doing Business with the United Arab Emirates.* GMB Publishing.

Thayer, Millie (2000) "Traveling Feminisms: From Embodied Women to Gendered Citizenship." In Global Ethnography: Forces, Connections, and Imaginations in a Postmodern World, edited by Michael Burawoy, Joseph A. Blum, Sheba George, Millie Thayer, Zsuzsa Gille, Teresa Gowan, Lynne

Haney, Maren Klawiter, Steve H. Lopez, and Sean Riain, 203–33. Berkeley: University of California Press.

Thomas, Hobbes (1953) *Leviathan*, intro. A. D. Lindsay. London: Dent and Sons; chaps. 13, 17–18, 21, 26; and Hobbes, De Cive; or, The Citizen, ed. Sterling P. Lamprecht (New York: Appleton-Century-Crofts, 1949), chaps. 1, 5–6, 13.

Thomas, Justin (2013) *Psychological Well-Being in the Gulf States: The New Arabia Felix*. UK: Palgrave Macmillan.

Togeby Lise (2008) 'The Political Representation of Ethnic Minorities Denmark as a Deviant Case', *Party Politics*, 14(3):325-343.

Touraine, Alain (2007) *New Paradigm for Understanding Today's World*. London: Polity.

Tripodi, Paolo and Belyeu, Grady (2005) "Whatever Happens to Somalia...Ignoring It Is No Longer an Option", *Low Intensity Conflict & Law Enforcement*, 13(3):212-226.

Turton, Edmond (1974) "The Isaq Somali Diaspora and Poll-Tax Agitation in Kenya 1936-41", *African Affairs*, 73(292) 325-346.

Umut, Erel (2010) "Migrating Cultural Capital: Bourdieu in Migration Studies", *Sociology* 44 (4): 642-660.

Valentini, Laura (2011) "A paradigm shift in theorizing about justice? A Critique of Sen?" *Economics and Philosophy*, 27 (3): 297-315.

Van, Amersfoort (2004) "Gabriel Sheffer and the Diaspora Experience", *Diaspora*, 13(2-3): 359-374.

Vatter, Miguel (2013) *Machiavelli's 'The Prince': A Reader's Guide*. London: Bloomsbury.

Vickers, Brendan (2012) "Towards a new aid paradigm: South Africa as African Development Partner" *Cambridge Review of International Affairs*, 25 (4):

Vincia, Anthony (2006) "An analysis and comparison of armed groups in Somalia", *African Security Review*, 15(1):75-90.

Walker, Chris (2014) "Somalia's security is tied to its natural resources: al-Shabaab's hold on conflict charcoal raises alarms": East Africa - issue in focus, *Africa Conflict Monthly Monitor*, 1(1):41-48.

Waters, Johanna (2003) "Flexible citizens? Transnationalism and citizenship amongst economic immigrants in Vancouver", *The Canadian Geographer/Le Géographe canadie*n, 47(3):219-234.

Weber, Max (2013) From Max Weber: Essays in sociology. Routledge.

Webersik, Christian (2005) "Fighting for the Plenty: The Banana Trade in Southern Somalia.". *Oxford Development Studies*, 33(1):81-97.

Weiss, Thomas (2009) (Ed.) "Migration for Development in the Horn of Africa Health expertise from the Somali diaspora in Finland". International Organization for Migration (IOM).

Werbner, Pnina (2000) "Divided loyalties, empowered citizenship? Muslims in Britain", *Citizenship Studies*, 4(3):307-324.

Williams, Melissa and Warren, Mark (2014). "A Democratic Case for Comparative Political Theory", *Political Theory*, 42:26.

Williams, Zack (2001) "No democracy, no development: reflections on democracy and development in Africa", *Review of African Political Economy*, 28 (88):213-223.

Wilson, Andrew (2014) *Ukraine Crisis: What it means for the West*. Yale University Press.

Wright, Derek (2002) (Ed.) "Emerging Perspectives on Nuruddin Farah." Asmara: Africa World Press, Inc.

Yanacopulos, Helen, and Matt Baillie Smith. (2007) "The ambivalent cosmopolitanism of international NGOs": 298-315.

Young, Joseph and Findley, Michael (2011) "Can peace be purchased? "A sectoral-level analysis of aid's influence on transnational terrorism", *Public Choice*, 149(3-4):365-381.

Zaidi Ali (2011) *Islam, Modernity, and the Human Sciences* (New York: Palgrave MacMillan, 2011), xvþ161 pp

Zank , Wolfgang (2014) "A "New Silk Road" between China and the Arab World" in Li Xing (ed.) *The BRICS and Beyond- The International Political Economy of the Emergence of a New World Order*. London: Ashgate.

Zekmi, Silvia (2010) Colonization Or Globalization?: Postcolonial Explorations of Imperial expansion, Lexington Books.

Index

A
Aalborg University, Denmark, iv, v
Action Aid, vi, 53, 235
Afghanistan, 145, 161
Agency, 21, 57, 129, 134, 176, 209, 226
Ahmed, Ali Jimale, iv, 17, 40, 55, 78, 96, 104, 105, 115, 128, 186, 217, 227, 235, 241, 250
Alienation, 155, 174
Amoud University, 11, 29, 85, 87, 88, 89, 92, 95, 97, 98, 101, 250
Arab Gulf, 85
Arabian Gulf, v, 18, 99, 166, 177
Arabian Peninsula, 51, 98, 184
Aristotle, 14
Authoritarian regimes, 162

B
Bakhtin, Mikhail, 210, 229
Battuta, Ibn, 50
Brazil, vi, 121, 126, 130, 133, 138, 167
BRICS, vi, 119, 120, 121, 123, 124, 125, 126, 127, 128, 129, 130, 131, 132, 135, 137, 138, 139, 235, 242, 245, 251, 253, 254, 257
Bureaucracy, 16, 24, 85

C
Capital, 19, 41, 42, 46, 52, 57, 64, 67, 68, 71, 73, 81, 87, 88, 89, 90, 91, 92, 94, 97, 98, 101, 106, 132, 148, 171, 175, 178, 180, 186, 187, 191, 198, 199, 201, 205, 210, 215, 221, 222, 226, 233
Cassanneli, Lee, 35, 36

Chen, Hongbing, iv
China, iv, v, vi, 9, 13, 27, 28, 118, 120, 121, 123, 126, 127, 128, 129, 130, 131, 133, 134, 135, 136, 137, 138, 139, 167, 168, 170, 192, 229, 231, 238, 240, 244, 246, 247, 250, 252, 254, 257
Ciid, 115
Civil war, 11, 12, 24, 29, 42, 43, 47, 57, 64, 80, 88, 93, 95, 96, 97, 113, 117, 162, 163, 181, 182, 187, 193, 197, 235
Cold War, 119, 125
Colonialism, 49, 60, 75, 76, 83, 131, 236, 244
Conflicts, 52, 76, 97, 147, 163, 169, 209
Congo, 167
Constitution, 42, 146, 151, 216, 225
Coordination, 55, 81
Corporations, 10, 128, 133, 136
Cosmopolitan, 21, 74, 94, 107, 111, 124, 163
Cross border, 25, 56
Cultural hubris, 208
Culture, iv, v, 228, 230, 231, 234, 236, 238, 239, 247
CUNY Graduate Center, New York, iv

D
Danish Radio, 41
Danood, 115
de Tocqueville, Alexis, 104

Democracy, 34, 119, 120, 127, 130, 132, 133, 145, 148, 227, 233, 236, 246, 256
Denmark, 15, 38, 57, 58, 90, 92, 201, 202, 203, 204, 205, 206, 207, 211, 213, 214, 216, 217, 220, 221, 222, 224, 225, 226, 228, 231, 234, 235, 237, 246, 247, 249, 253, 255
Diaspora, 46, 51, 55, 56, 57, 58, 59, 61, 228, 229, 231, 233, 235, 238, 239, 247, 248, 251, 252, 253, 255
Diaspora NGOs, 56
Diasporic transnational interest groups, 106
Diplomacy, 136, 240, 254
Dubai, 186
Durkheim, Emile, 173, 237

E

East Africa, 27, 64, 256
Emerging powers, 14, 120, 126, 131, 135, 138, 170, 246
Emirates, 193
Empowerment, 12, 18, 47, 55, 56, 59, 73, 88, 136, 199, 201, 204
Entrepreneurship, 18, 117, 163, 175, 183, 186, 191, 193, 222
Esmann, Frank, 41, 42
Essentialization, 71
Ethnicity, 103, 152, 153, 156, 210
European colonization, 77, 108
Exclusion, 15, 56, 153, 155, 169, 175, 178, 189, 198, 199, 200, 202, 206, 208, 212, 213, 214, 215, 221, 225, 226, 245
Extraterritorial power, 154
Extremism, 18, 85, 87, 103, 110, 113, 141, 143, 144, 145, 146, 155, 157, 158, 160, 161, 164, 165, 168, 169, 170, 171

F

Facebook, 90, 92
Ferguson, James, 12, 20, 235
Field work, v, 176
Foucault, Michel, 176, 179, 236
Fragile states, 145
Freedom, 56, 57, 65, 78, 82, 114, 132, 134, 167
Fukuyama, Francis, 28, 119

G

Giri, Ananta, iv, 28, 44, 176, 236
Globalization, 31, 79, 109, 149, 152, 153, 225, 236, 247
Governance, 12, 93, 95, 119, 146, 162, 169, 171
Government, 41, 43, 70, 73, 87, 112, 113, 114, 150, 152, 163, 182, 183, 189, 191, 195, 197, 202, 219, 220, 221, 222, 223, 224, 254
Gramsci, Antonio, 86, 124, 134, 229, 239, 243
Grassroots transnationalism, 120

H

Habermas, Jürgen, 66, 89, 119, 204, 208, 209, 237, 238
Hannah, Arendt, 229
Hervik, Peter, iv, 203, 204, 206, 212, 213, 239
Hobbes, Thomas, 48, 141, 255
Homeland, 15, 20, 57, 58, 59, 79, 80, 81, 91, 109, 116, 151, 152, 155, 169, 178, 179, 180, 181, 182, 184, 186, 187, 188, 189, 190, 191, 192, 193, 194, 195, 196, 197, 198, 200, 247
Hong Kong, 125

Horn of Africa, v, 9, 11, 17, 18, 27, 85, 91, 101, 111, 143, 158, 161, 164, 168, 170, 191, 199, 243, 256
Host country, 57, 91, 155, 178, 180, 181, 188, 190, 192, 194, 195, 196, 197, 198

I

Identity, 20, 33, 54, 55, 56, 79, 89, 108, 136, 145, 151, 153, 154, 156, 169, 177, 180, 182, 189, 202, 203, 204, 208, 209, 210, 211, 217, 224, 246, 252
Inclusion, 34, 118, 148, 164, 166, 189, 206, 208, 209, 210, 213
Indian Ocean, 27, 228
Innovative, 59, 89
Iowa State University, iv

J

Jihad, 78, 114

K

Kenya, 191, 255
Kinship relations, 187
Kusow, Abdi, iv

L

Labour, 65, 75, 77, 132, 154, 173, 175, 184, 185, 194, 195, 201, 223, 247, 252
Libya, 145, 161

M

Madras Institute of Development Studies, India, iv
Majority, 97, 131, 145, 177, 213, 237
Makeshift schools, 117
Mamdani, Mahmood, 36, 49, 88, 167, 244
Mazrui, 37, 77, 105, 108, 115, 244, 245
Mazrui, Ali, 174
Meso structures, 65
Micro-credits, 58
Middle East, 9, 11, 28, 64, 119, 121, 122, 123, 125, 126, 127, 128, 130, 133, 136, 137, 139, 199, 238, 239, 243
Minorities, 14, 59, 75, 123, 211, 213, 216, 221, 222, 237
Mobility, 13, 14, 18, 19, 48, 89, 90, 92, 93, 100, 121, 149, 153, 154, 173, 174, 175, 180, 182, 183, 200, 232, 240, 252
Mobilization, 40, 46, 54, 55, 57, 61, 76, 78, 82, 104, 114, 116, 118, 153, 202, 205, 215, 224, 226, 235
Modernity, 25, 229, 257
Mogadishu, v, 41, 42, 49, 81, 95, 101, 111, 112, 113, 163, 228
Mohamed, Mohamed, 35, 37, 78, 95, 112, 114, 115, 132, 227, 241, 246
Moral, ii, 33, 53, 67, 90, 124
Multicultural, 156
Muslim country, 145

N

Nation, 15, 19
Nationalism, 14, 20, 60, 78, 79, 81, 105, 157, 179, 204, 216, 225, 239, 246
Neoliberal, 183
Neo-liberalization, 183
Networks, v, 20, 21, 25, 52, 54, 67, 71, 73, 89, 90, 92, 153, 157, 176, 178, 180, 186, 188, 195, 196, 207, 224, 241, 247, 253
NGOs, vi, 20, 31, 37, 42, 45, 46, 51, 52, 53, 54, 58, 59, 60, 91, 96,

100, 114, 117, 121, 123, 124, 126, 128, 129, 130, 132, 134, 139, 227, 243, 246, 257
Non-State Actors, 238
North America, 186, 194, 197, 199
North-Western University, Shenyang, China, iv, v

O

Opposition, 49, 68, 77, 80, 87, 106, 108, 158, 213, 220, 224
Oratory, 78, 114
Organization, vi, 256
Ottoman Empire, 93
Oxfam, vi, 53, 237

P

Parochialisation, 17
Partnership, 58, 125, 136
Personal, 48, 72, 81, 99, 107, 151, 160, 166
Plural, 203, 233
Populism, 201, 202, 203, 204, 212, 218, 225, 226
Precarity, 15, 174, 175, 176, 182, 183, 186
Projects, 16, 20, 47, 53, 57, 58, 99, 100, 104, 111, 127, 129, 135, 160, 168
Public discourse, 122
Public sphere, 22, 31, 66, 70, 71, 209, 210, 230
Puntland, 51, 113, 163, 170, 193
Putnam, Robert, 67, 68, 71, 87, 205, 248

Q

qabiil, 187, 189

R

Reconciliation, 11, 41, 42, 44, 61, 80, 151, 159, 231, 235

Red Green Alliance, 215
Red Sea, 192
Regional, 11, 12, 18, 24, 38, 51, 61, 64, 72, 74, 79, 80, 81, 82, 96, 98, 100, 106, 113, 115, 151, 155, 163, 165, 170, 177, 188, 192, 193, 197
Regionalism, 83
Religion, 33, 103, 117, 152, 155, 170, 202, 208
Remittance, 57, 58, 154, 180, 182, 190, 191, 192, 198
Responsibility, 33, 37, 49, 53, 111, 155, 209
Revolution, 236

S

Scandinavian countries, 27
Second World War, 95, 148
Secular, 36, 47, 66, 79, 94, 95, 107, 108, 208
Sen, Amartya, 15, 32, 33, 36, 145, 167, 201, 203, 204, 208, 209, 220, 236, 251, 255
Sharjah, 191
Simmel, George, 177, 207, 252
Social cohesion, 178, 208
Social cohesion., 178
Social movements, 34, 254
Social theory, 204
Socialist People's Party, 214, 218
Societal, 36, 40, 45, 49, 52, 63, 107, 166, 178
Somali Diaspora, 154, 190, 191, 192, 255
Somali NGOs, 59
Somaliland, 51, 113, 152, 163, 170, 193, 235

T

Transformation, 71, 124, 144, 238, 248, 250
Transnational communities, 9, 10, 11, 13, 14, 15, 20, 21, 22, 27, 28, 29, 32, 34, 51, 55, 79, 80, 81, 82, 83, 91, 93, 96, 97, 98, 99, 101, 109, 116, 118, 144, 145, 146, 152, 153, 154, 155, 156, 157, 166, 168, 169, 171, 175, 176, 179, 180, 183, 190, 191, 192, 193, 194, 195, 196, 198, 199, 200
Transnational Connections, 25, 152, 238
Transnational NGOs, v, 32, 34, 46, 50, 51, 52, 53, 54, 55, 58, 59, 61, 85, 91, 93, 96, 100, 101, 124, 134, 141, 142, 160, 167
Traore, Karim, ii
Turkey, 66, 85, 111, 118, 135, 167, 227

U

Ukraine, 125, 256
Ulama, 11, 90, 91, 96, 97, 101
Unilateral Declaration of Superiority, 161
United Emirates, 182
United States, 113, 157, 233, 246
Universities, v, 94, 95
USSR., 125

V

Vicious cycle of resentment, 40
Virtual ethnographic methodology, 90, 92
Visionary leadership, 99

W

Warlordism, 78
Weak states, 110, 157
Weber, Max, 16, 22, 33, 86, 131, 229, 256
Welfare, 149
Welfare systems, 209, 211
Western TNGOs, 124, 126, 132
Westphalia, 131, 147
Women activists, 106
World Bank, 53, 237
WWII decolonization, 149

Y

Yemen, 189

www.ingramcontent.com/pod-product-compliance
Lightning Source LLC
Chambersburg PA
CBHW062012220426
43662CB00010B/1295